1

FOCUS
ON
GRAMMAR
AN INTEGRATED SKILLS APPROACH

SECOND EDITION

D1305877

LIDA BAKER

PEARSON
Longman

FOCUS ON GRAMMAR 1: An Integrated Skills Approach
Teacher's Manual

Pearson Education, 10 Bank Street, White Plains, NY 10606

Staff credits: The people who made up the *Focus on Grammar 1 Teacher's Manual* team,
representing editorial, production, design, and manufacturing, are: Rhea Banker, John
Barnes, Nancy Blodgett, Christine Edmonds, Nancy Flaggman, Ann France, Laura
Le Dréan, Mindy DePalma, and Laurie Neaman.
Cover images: background: Comstock Images; background shell and center shell: Nick
Koudis
Text composition: ElectraGraphics, Inc.
Text font: 11/13 Sabon, 10/13 Myriad Roman

ISBN: 0-13-147468-5

LONGMAN ON THE **WEB**

Longman.com offers online resources for
teachers and students. Access our Companion
Websites, our online catalog, and our local
offices around the world.

Visit us at **longman.com.**

Printed in the United States of America
2 3 4 5 6 7 8 9 10—BAH—12 11 10 09 08 07

Contents

Contents

Introduction

The *Focus on Grammar* series

Written by ESL/EFL professionals, *Focus on Grammar: An Integrated Skills Approach* helps students to understand and practice English grammar. The primary aim of the course is for students to gain confidence in their ability to speak and write English accurately and fluently.

The new edition retains this popular series' focus on English grammar through lively listening, speaking, reading, and writing activities. The new *Focus on Grammar* also maintains the same five-level progression as the second edition:

- Level 1 (Beginning, formerly Introductory)
- Level 2 (High-Beginning, formerly Basic)
- Level 3 (Intermediate)
- Level 4 (High-Intermediate)
- Level 5 (Advanced)

What is the *Focus on Grammar* methodology?

Both controlled and communicative practice

While students expect and need to learn the formal rules of a language, it is crucial that they also practice new structures in a variety of contexts in order to internalize and master them. To this end, *Focus on Grammar* provides an abundance of both controlled and communicative exercises so that students can bridge the gap between knowing grammatical structures and using them. The many communicative activities in each Student Book unit provide opportunities for critical thinking while enabling students to personalize what they have learned.

A unique four-step approach

The series follows a four-step approach:

Step 1: Grammar in Context shows the new structures in natural contexts, such as articles and conversations.

Step 2: Grammar Presentation presents the structures in clear and accessible grammar charts, notes, and examples.

Step 3: Focused Practice of both form and meaning of the new structures is provided in numerous and varied controlled exercises.

Step 4: Communication Practice allows students to use the new structures freely and creatively in motivating, open-ended activities.

Thorough recycling

Underpinning the scope and sequence of the *Focus on Grammar* series is the belief that students need to use target structures many times, in different contexts, and at increasing levels of difficulty. For this reason, new grammar is constantly recycled throughout the book so that students have maximum exposure to the target forms and become comfortable using them in speech and in writing.

A complete classroom text and reference guide

A major goal in the development of *Focus on Grammar* has been to provide students with books that serve not only as vehicles for classroom instruction but also as resources for reference and self-study. In each Student Book, the combination of grammar charts, grammar notes, a glossary of grammar terms, and extensive appendices provides a complete and invaluable reference guide for students.

Ongoing assessment

Review Tests at the end of each part of the Student Book allow for self-assessment. In addition, the tests in the new *Focus on Grammar* Assessment Package provide teachers with a valid, reliable, and practical means of determining students' appropriate levels of placement in the course and of assessing students' achievement throughout the course. At Levels 4 (High-Intermediate) and 5 (Advanced), Proficiency Tests give teachers an overview of their students' general grammar knowledge.

What are the components of each level of *Focus on Grammar*?

Student Book

The Student Book is divided into eight or more parts, depending on the level. Each part contains grammatically related units, with each unit focusing on specific grammatical structures; where appropriate, units present contrasting forms. The exercises in each unit are thematically related to one another, and all units have the same clear, easy-to-follow format.

Teacher's Manual

The Teacher's Manual contains a variety of suggestions and information to enrich the material in the Student Book. It includes general teaching suggestions for each section of a typical unit, answers to frequently asked questions, unit-by-unit teaching tips with ideas for further communicative practice, and a supplementary activity section. Answers to the Student Book exercises and audioscripts of the listening activities are found at the back of the Teacher's Manual. Also included in the Teacher's Manual is a CD-ROM that includes PowerPoint® presentations that offer alternative ways of presenting selected grammar structures.

Workbook

The Workbook accompanying each level of *Focus on Grammar* provides additional exercises for self-study of the target grammar for each unit. Tests included in each Workbook provide students with additional opportunities for self-assessment.

Audio Programs

The Student Book Class Audio Program includes the listening activities, the Grammar in Context passages, and various other exercises. The symbol ⌒ identifies audio for the listening exercises. The symbol ⌒ next to the Grammar in Context passages and other exercises indicates that the listening is optional. Audioscripts for the listening exercises are located in the back of the Teacher's Manual.

Some Student Books are packaged with a Student Audio CD. This CD includes the listening exercise from each unit.

CD-ROM

The *Focus on Grammar* CD-ROM provides students with individualized practice and immediate feedback. Fully contextualized and interactive, the activities extend practice of the grammatical structures in the reading, writing, speaking, and listening skills areas. The CD-ROM includes grammar review, review tests, score-based remedial practice, games, and all relevant reference material from the Student Book. It can also be used in conjunction with the *Longman Interactive American Dictionary* CD-ROM.

Assessment Package (NEW)

A comprehensive Assessment Package has been developed for each level of the new edition of *Focus on Grammar*. The components of the Assessment Package are:

1. **Placement, Diagnostic, and Achievement Tests**

   - a Placement Test to screen students and place them into the correct level
   - Diagnostic Tests for each part of the Student Book
   - Unit Achievement Tests for each unit of the Student Book
   - Part Achievement Tests for each part of the Student Book

2. **General Proficiency Tests**

   - two Proficiency Tests at Level 4 (High-Intermediate)
   - two Proficiency Tests at Level 5 (Advanced)

   These tests can be administered at any point in the course.

3. **Audio CD**

   - Audio CDs include the listening portions of the Placement, Diagnostic, and Achievement Tests.
   - The audioscripts for the tests are located in the Assessment Package.

4. **Test-Generating Software**

   The test-bank software provides thousands of questions from which teachers can create class-appropriate tests. All items are labeled according to the grammar structure they are testing, so teachers can easily select relevant items; they can also design their own items to add to their tests.

Transparencies (NEW)

Transparencies of all the grammar charts in the Student Book are also available. These transparencies are classroom visual aids that help instructors point out and explain important patterns and structures of grammar.

Companion Website

The *Focus on Grammar* companion website (www. longman.com/focusongrammar) contains a wealth of information and activities for both teachers and students. In addition to general information about the course pedagogy, the website provides extensive practice exercises for the classroom, a language lab, or at home.

What's new in this edition of the Student Book?

In response to users' requests, this edition has:

- a new four-color design
- easy-to-read color coding for the four steps
- new and updated reading texts for Grammar in Context
- more exercise items
- an editing (error analysis) exercise in each unit
- From Grammar to Writing exercises for each part
- a Glossary of Grammar terms
- expanded Appendices

References

Alexander, L. G. (1988). *Longman English Grammar*. White Plains, NY: Longman.

Biber, D., S. Conrad, E. Finegan, S. Johansson, and G. Leech (1999). *Longman Grammar of Spoken and Written English*. White Plains, NY: Longman.

Celce-Murcia, M., and D. Freeman (1999). *The Grammar Book*. Boston: Heinle and Heinle.

Celce-Murcia, M., and S. Hilles (1988). *Techniques and Resources in Teaching Grammar*. New York: Oxford University Press.

Firsten, R. (2002). *The ELT Grammar Book*. Burlingame, CA: Alta Book Center Publishers.

Garner, B. (2003). *Garner's Modern American Usage*. New York: Oxford University Press.

Greenbaum, S. (1996). *The Oxford English Grammar*. New York: Oxford University Press.

Leech, G. (2004). *Meaning and the English Verb*. Harlow, UK: Pearson.

Lewis, M. (1997). *Implementing the Lexical Approach*. Hove, East Sussex, UK: Language Teaching Publications.

Longman (2002). *Longman Dictionary of English Language and Culture*. Harlow, UK: Longman.

Willis, D. (2003). *Rules, Patterns, and Words*. New York: Cambridge University Press.

About the *Focus on Grammar* Teacher's Manual

This Teacher's Manual offers a multitude of ideas for working with the material in *Focus on Grammar 1: An Integrated Skills Approach,* second edition. In this manual, you will find the following information:

• **General Teaching Tips** (pages 1–12) describe the principles underlying the course and give suggestions for teaching the activities in the Student Book. A Strategies for Teaching Grammar page offers a quick reference for some of the most common and useful grammar teaching techniques. A Frequently Asked Questions section answers some of the most common issues encountered by teachers.

• **Unit-by-Unit Teaching Tips** (pages 13–88) give you additional ideas for completing the activities unique to each unit.

• **Supplementary Activities** (pages 89–92) provide extra practice exercises for use during your presentation of a grammar point.

• **Audioscripts** and the **Student Book Answer Key** are included at the back of the Teacher's Manual for easy reference.

The **PowerPoint® presentations CD-ROM** bound into this Teacher's Manual includes additional teaching tools and resources:

• **PowerPoint® presentations** for selected units in the Student Book offer an innovative method for the contextualized instruction of grammar. These theme-based, user-friendly presentations contain a variety of colorful graphics and animations to engage a wide range of learning styles. In addition to providing a stimulating visual reinforcement of the Grammar Notes, these presentations also include interactive practice activities.

• A **PowerPoint® presentation guide,** included on the CD-ROM in PDF format, offers guidelines for using the **PowerPoint® presentations.** It contains a variety of suggestions for getting the most out of the presentations in terms of both instructional benefit and learner participation.

• **Transparencies** of all Grammar Charts in the Student Book offer an additional teaching tool for presenting the target grammar points in the classroom.

General Teaching Tips

These tips are designed to guide you in teaching the recurring sections of the Teacher's Manual and Student Book. Experimenting with the various options will enliven your classroom and appeal to students' different learning styles.

In the following section the icon ⏱ indicates an optional step you may wish to include if time permits.

Unit Overview

The Unit Overview (offered in the Teacher's Manual) highlights the most important grammar points of each unit. You may also find it helpful to review the Grammar Charts and Grammar Notes in the Student Book before teaching each unit.

Grammar in Context

Each unit of the Student Book begins with a reading selection designed to raise students' interest and expose them to the target grammar in a realistic, natural context. The selections include conversations, e-mail messages, and other formats that students may encounter in their day-to-day lives. All of the texts are also available on the Audio Program.

Background Notes

Where appropriate, background notes are provided in the Teacher's Manual to explain cultural and historical terms or concepts that appear in a reading selection. You can introduce these terms and concepts to students during a warm-up discussion, or you can use the notes as a reference if questions come up as students are reading.

Reading (15–25 minutes)

Depending on the needs of your class, have students complete the reading in class or at home (procedures for both options are given below). Whichever option you choose,

encourage students (1) to read with a purpose; (2) to read the passage through once or twice without stopping for unknown words; and (3) to identify and deal with new vocabulary.

Comprehension questions and discussion topics are offered in the Unit-by-Unit Teaching Tips to supplement the grammar-focused activities of the Student Book.

Suggested Procedure for Reading

1. Play the audio and have students follow along in their books.
2. Write the comprehension questions from the Unit-by-Unit Teaching Tips on the board.
3. Have students read the passage again silently, looking for answers to the questions.
4. ⏱ Have students discuss their answers with a partner or in small groups.
5. Call on individuals to share their answers with the class.
6. ⏱ Put students in pairs or small groups to discuss the reading. Invite them to respond to the reading in a way that is meaningful to them: What was most interesting? What did they learn?

Option A (At Home/In Class)

- Write the comprehension questions on the board for students to copy, or prepare them as a handout for students to take home.
- Have students read the passage and answer the questions at home.
- ⏱ Have students write a few additional questions about the reading.
- In class, have students work in pairs or small groups to discuss their answers.
- ⏱ Have students take turns asking and answering questions they prepared at home.
- Follow steps 5–6 in the Suggested Procedure for Reading above.

Option B (In Class)

- Have students work in pairs. Divide the reading in half, and have each student in the pair read one half.

- Have students summarize the information in their half of the reading for their partner.
- Follow steps 5–6 in the previous notes for Suggested Procedure for Reading.

Words and Expressions (15–25 minutes)

Suggested Procedure for Words and Expressions

1. Have students first listen to and repeat the words and expressions.
2. Have students practice the short conversations with a partner. Encourage them to use body language whenever possible.
3. Encourage students to keep a record of words and expressions by using a notebook or by making vocabulary cards. The entries should include a definition and an example sentence. Suggest that they be on the lookout for other examples of these items and add any new examples they find to their notebooks or cards.

Where appropriate, encourage students to draw pictures on the card or to record any information that helps them remember the vocabulary item. It may be helpful for students to include a translation of the new word or expression in their own language.

Here's one way to do a vocabulary card:

		[front]
	thrill (n., v.)	

[back]
(n) a strong feeling of excitement or
pleasure (My grandmother always gets a
thrill when I call her.)
(v) to feel or make someone feel strong
excitement or pleasure (The skaters **thrilled**
their fans with their high jumps.)

Working Together (10–20 minutes)

These activities help students focus indirectly on the meaning of the target grammar while talking about the world they know.

Suggested Procedure for Working Together

1. Have students work in pairs or groups to practice the conversation or reading. Encourage them to imitate the intonation used on the audio program. You may wish to highlight certain stress and intonation patterns by having students listen and repeat.
2. Whenever possible, have students switch roles.
3. Call on volunteers to read segments of the text for the class.
4. When appropriate, after students complete the final part of the exercise, extend the practice by personalizing the activity. In Unit 9, for example, after students talk about the Williams sisters and the princes, encourage them to go on and talk about other famous siblings. A follow-up activity would be for students to bring photos of famous siblings for classmates to identify.

Grammar Presentation

There are many ways to teach the material in the Grammar Presentation. As a general rule, the more varied and lively the classroom activities, the more engaged students will be—and the more learning will occur! Approaching grammar from different angles and trying out different classroom management options can help increase student motivation.

The Strategies for Teaching Grammar on page 8 provides some guidelines to keep in mind when presenting a new grammar point. In addition to these strategies and the procedures outlined below, you can find specific suggestions for presenting the unit's grammar in the Unit-by-Unit Teaching Tips.

Identify the Grammar (5–10 minutes)

This section in the Teacher's Manual provides support for you to help students identify the target grammatical structures embedded in the reading. This helps students learn the usage of the target grammar point and helps you make a smooth transition from Grammar in Context to the Grammar Presentation.

Suggested Procedure for Identify the Grammar

1. Choose an example of the target grammar from the reading and write it on the board. The Unit-by-Unit Teaching Tips provide examples that focus on specific features of that grammar point.
2. Point out that the target grammar is presented in boldfaced type in the reading for easy identification. Elicit more examples from students and write them on the board.
3. Find out what your students may already know about that grammar point. List the information you have elicited on the board. As students continue with the Grammar Presentation, encourage them to compare these notes with the information presented in the Grammar Charts and Grammar Notes.

After studying the grammar in context, students should be ready to study the isolated forms, meanings, and usage. You can use the charts, notes, and examples to present and review the grammatical structures in a straightforward and comprehensive way.

Note that common grammatical terms are used throughout the Grammar Presentations because they help make the explanations clearer and because students often have learned them in their own language. If students are having trouble understanding the grammatical terms, encourage them to use the Glossary provided in the back of the Student Book.

Grammar Charts (5–10 minutes)

The Grammar Charts provide a clear reference of all the forms of the target grammar. Students also become familiar with grammatical terminology. The charts also enable you to pre-teach some of the Grammar Notes that follow. In addition to the charts in the Student Book, you may want to use the Focus on Grammar Transparencies (on the CD-ROM in the back of this Teacher's Manual) to help direct all of your students' attention to the same focus point.

Suggested Procedure for Grammar Charts

1. Using the examples you wrote on the board (see Identify the Grammar above) and/or Focus on Grammar Transparencies, draw students' attention to important features in the models by asking them questions or by pointing out the key features.

2. Confirm students' understanding by engaging them in some recognition activities. Try one or two activities from Strategies 3, 4, 5, or 6 (page 8).
3. Get students to manipulate the new structures through substitution or transformation drills. See Strategy 7 (page 8) for an example of a transformation drill.
4. Encourage students to make sentences that are personally meaningful using the new grammar.

Option A
• Have students study the Grammar Charts at home.
• In class, follow step 1 in the suggested procedure above.
• Move directly to the Grammar Notes section. Carry out steps 2, 3, and 4 in the suggested procedure above using the notes together with the charts.

Option B
• Assign individual students responsibility for presenting a topic to the class by combining the information in the charts and the relevant notes. Give them newsprint (a large piece of paper) and a marker to prepare a display in class or at home.
• ⏱ Meet with students individually. Allow them to rehearse their presentations and provide any coaching needed.
• Call on students to present their topics to the class. Encourage class questions.
• Choose appropriate practice activities from Strategies 4–8 (page 8) OR move directly to the Grammar Notes section.

Grammar Notes (10–30 minutes)

These notes provide helpful information about the meaning, use, and form of the grammatical structures that students have encountered in the introductory reading selection and Grammar Charts. They include the following features to help students understand and use the forms.
• Where appropriate, time lines illustrate the meaning of verb forms and their relationship to one another.
• *Be careful!* notes alert students to common errors among English language learners.
• Additional *Notes* provide information about spelling, meaning, and usage.
• *Pronunciation Notes* are provided when appropriate.

- Below the notes and examples, references to related units and appendices are provided.

The Grammar Notes section includes cross-references to the Focused Practice exercises in the Student Book and to the Supplementary Activities in this Teacher's Manual. Have students complete the appropriate exercises after you present each note. This breaks up the grammar presentation into manageable chunks and allows students to check their understanding of the note.

Suggested Procedure for Grammar Notes

1. Have students read each note at home and/or in class.
2. For each note, write examples on the board and elicit from students the important features of the form (see Strategy 1, page 8, for suggestions) or point out the key features yourself.
3. If possible, demonstrate the meaning of the grammatical form(s) by performing actions (see Strategy 6, page 8).
4. Model the examples and have students repeat after you so that they become comfortable with the appropriate stress, intonation, and rhythm.
5. Engage students with the grammar point by choosing appropriate activities, for example:
   - Elicit examples of the target structure.
   - Confirm students' understanding by having them categorize examples or perform actions that illustrate structure. See Strategies 5 and 6 (page 8) for examples.
   - Provide controlled practice with quick substitution or transformation drills.
   - Encourage students to make personally meaningful sentences using the new grammatical forms.
   - Use the Focused Practice exercises in the Student Book and/or the Supplementary Activities starting on page 89 of this Teacher's Manual.
6. You may want to repeat steps 2–5 for each Grammar Note. Where appropriate, the Unit-by-Unit Teaching Tips give suggestions for presenting two or more notes simultaneously.

Option

- Photocopy one set of Grammar Notes for each group of three or four students in your class. Cut them up so that the notes and their corresponding examples are not attached.

- Divide the class into groups of three or four students and give a set of cut-up notes to each group.
- Give students their task:
  1. Match the examples with the correct notes.
  2. Attach the notes and corresponding examples to a sheet of newsprint (a large piece of paper).
  3. Have students create more examples for each note.
- Circulate to ensure that students are on the right track, and provide help as needed.
- Have students post their results around the room, and invite groups to look at each other's work.
- Regroup as a whole class to answer questions.

Focused Practice

The exercises in this section provide practice for the structures in the Grammar Presentation. You may wish to have students complete each exercise immediately after you have presented the relevant Grammar Note. Another option is for students to complete one or more of the exercises at home, using the cross-references to the Grammar Note(s) for support.

If you decide to have students complete the exercises in class, you can keep them motivated by varying the order of the exercises and/or the way you conduct them. Following are various ways of conducting the exercises. In the Unit-by-Unit Teaching Tips, you will find definitions for potentially unfamiliar words and phrases that appear in the Focused Practice exercises.

Discover the Grammar (5–10 minutes)

This opening activity gets students to identify the target grammar structures in a realistic context. This recognition-only activity raises awareness of the structures as it builds confidence.

Suggested Procedure for Discover the Grammar

1. Go over the example with the class.
2. Have students complete the exercise individually or in pairs.
3. Elicit the correct answers from students.

Controlled Practice Exercises (5–10 minutes each)

Following the Discover the Grammar activity are exercises that provide practice in a controlled, but still contextualized, environment. The exercises proceed from simpler to more complex and include a variety of exercise types such as fill in the blanks, matching, and multiple-choice. Exercises are cross-referenced to the appropriate Grammar Notes so that students can review as necessary. Students are exposed to many different written formats, including letters, notes, e-mail messages, charts, and graphs. Many exercises are art-based, providing a rich context for meaningful practice.

Options
- Have students work in pairs to complete the exercises.
- If the exercise is in the form of a conversation, have students complete the exercise and then work in pairs to practice and perform the conversation for the class.
- When going over answers with students, have them explain why each answer is correct.
- Whenever possible, relate exercises to students' own lives. For example, if an exercise includes a time line, elicit from students some important events that have happened in their own lives.

Editing (10 minutes)

All units include an editing exercise to build students' awareness of incorrect usage of the target grammar structures. Students identify and correct errors in a contextualized passage such as a student's composition, a letter, or an online message-board posting. The direction line indicates the number of errors in the passage.

Suggested Procedure for Editing
1. Have students read through the passage quickly to understand its context and meaning.
2. Tell students to read the passage line by line, circling incorrect structures and writing in the corrections.
3. Have students take turns reading the passage line by line, saying the structures correctly. Alternatively, read the passage aloud to the class and have students interrupt you with their corrections.

4. There are also usually correct usages of the structures in each editing exercise. After students have identified the errors, point out the correct usages and ask why they are not errors.

Communication Practice

These in-class exercises give students the opportunity to use the target structure in communicative activities. These activities help develop listening and speaking fluency and critical thinking skills, as well as provide opportunities for students to "own" the structures. As with the Focused Practice exercises, you may wish to vary the order of these activities to keep student motivation high.

Since there are many different exercise types in the Communication Practice section, specific ideas and guidelines are provided in the Unit-by-Unit Teaching Tips. Following are general suggestions for the three main types of exercises. (Note: See the FAQ on pages 10–12 for more information about setting up pair work and group work.)

Listening (10 minutes)

Each Communication Practice section begins with a listening and a comprehension exercise. Students hear a variety of listening formats, including conversations, telephone messages, news broadcasts, and interviews. After listening, students complete a task that focuses on the form or meaning of the target grammar structure. The listening exercises are included on the Student CD so that students may also complete these exercises outside of class.

Suggested Procedure for Listening
Before students listen
1. Explain the situation or context of the listening passage. Provide any necessary cultural information, and pre-teach any vocabulary that students may need to know. Definitions are provided in the Unit-by-Unit Teaching Tips for words and phrases that may be unfamiliar to students. (Note that some of these words and phrases may appear in the listening, not in the exercise itself.)
2. Ask students to read the exercise questions so that they know what to listen for.

Listening

1. Play the audio or read the audioscript aloud. If you choose to read:
   - Speak with a lot of expression and at a natural pace.
   - Change positions and tone of voice to indicate who the speaker is. Another method is to draw stick figures on the board and label them with the characters' names so that you can point to the appropriate character as you change roles.
2. Have students listen the first time with their pencils down.
3. Have students listen again and complete the task.
4. You may want to let students listen as many times as necessary to complete the task.

After students listen

1. Elicit answers for the exercise items and write them on the board. Answer any questions the students may have.
2. ⏱ Students listen a final time and review the passage.

Option A
- Make photocopies of the audioscript and hand it out to students.
- Play the audio recording and have students read along with it in chorus. Explain that this exercise will help them to hear and practice the rhythms, stresses, and clusters of English sounds.

Option B
Have students listen and complete the exercise at home or in a language lab.

Role Plays (10–20 minutes)

In these classroom speaking activities, students role-play a real-life encounter, such as an interview.

Advantages of Role Plays
- They are fun and motivating for most students.
- Role-playing characters often allows the more hesitant students to be more outgoing than if they are speaking as themselves.
- By broadening the world of the classroom to the world outside, role-playing allows students to use a wider range of language than less open-ended activities.

Suggested Procedure for Role Plays
1. When possible, bring in props or costumes to add drama and fun.

2. Review the task so students understand what is required.
3. Perform a sample role play with a volunteer in front of the class.
4. Divide the class into the suggested groupings and give them a fixed time limit for completing the task.
5. Have students write a script for the role play. Then have them write key words on cards and perform the role play using the cards as prompts. Or have students plan the action without a script and present it extemporaneously.
6. While students are working, circulate among the pairs or groups to answer students' questions and help them with the activity.
7. Have various pairs or groups perform their role plays in front of the class. If possible, tape-record or videotape the role plays for students' own listening or viewing.

Information Gaps (10–20 minutes)

These games are designed to encourage communication between students. In these activities, each student has a different set of information. Students have to talk to their partners to find facts, provide definitions, or identify famous tourist destinations.

Advantages of Information Gaps
- Like role plays, information gaps are motivating and fun.
- Information gaps are additionally motivating because there is a real need for communication in order to combine the information to solve a problem and complete the task.
- Information sharing allows students to extend and personalize what they have learned in the unit.

Suggested Procedure for Information Gaps
1. Explain how the Student A and Student B pages relate to each other (how they are different or similar).
2. Refer students to the examples and to any language provided.
3. Divide the class into pairs (Student A and Student B) and have them position themselves so that they cannot see the contents of each other's books.
4. Tell the Student Bs what page to turn to, and circulate to check that they are looking at the correct page.
5. Have students read their separate instructions. Check comprehension of the

task by asking each group, "What are you going to do?"

6. Remind students not to show each other the contents of their pages.

7. As students are working, circulate to answer individual questions and to help students with the activity.

Further Practice

A Further Practice activity (in the Teacher's Manual only) can be found at the end of every unit in the Unit-by-Unit Teaching Tips. These exercises offer additional communicative practice with the target structure of the unit. Most can be done in class with no before-class preparation.

GRAMMAR OUT OF THE BOX......

This activity (in the Teacher's Manual only) offers ideas for how to bring "real life" into your grammar classroom. Using video, pictures, news articles, or other realia, these activities help students make the connection between the structures they learn in the classroom and their application in the real world.

Review Test

The last section of each Part of the Student Book is a review feature that can be used as a self-test. These exercises test the form and use of the grammar content presented and practiced in that Part. They give students a chance to check their knowledge and to review any problematic areas before moving on to the next part. An Answer Key is provided at the back of the Student Book, with cross-references to units for easy review.

Suggested Procedure for Review Test

1. Have students complete the exercises at home and check their answers in the Answer Key.

2. During the next class, go over any remaining questions students may have.

Option

• Have students complete the exercises in class. Give them a time limit of 20–30 minutes and circulate as they work.

• Have students use the Answer Key to check and correct their answers in pairs. Alternatively, go over the answers as a class.

From Grammar to Writing

The From Grammar to Writing section at the back of the Student Book has a writing activity for each Part of the Student Book that includes a grammar point and relates this grammar point to the writing focus. Students may practice the teaching point in a controlled exercise such as a fill-in or identification. Students may also practice pre-writing strategies such as making charts or Venn diagrams. Finally, students apply the teaching point in a writing task. Text types include personal letters, notes, and e-mail messages.

Suggested Procedure for From Grammar to Writing

Pre-writing

1. Where a controlled practice exercise occurs, have students work individually to complete the exercise. Then have them exchange books and compare answers.

2. Go over the answers as a class and answer any questions that students have at this point.

3. Where a pre-writing task occurs, explain the task to students. Where appropriate, provide a model for students on the board or on an overhead.

4. Have students work in pairs or small groups to complete the pre-writing task. Circulate while they are working to answer any questions and help them with the activity.

Composing and Correcting

1. Go over the requirements of the assignment to make sure students understand what they are expected to do.

2. Have students complete the writing assignment at home.

3. ⏲ Have students revise their writing and turn in the second draft to you.

Option

• Have students complete the controlled practice exercise(s) at home.

• In class, have students work in pairs to compare answers.

• Follow the suggested procedure above, starting from step 4 in the pre-writing phase.

Strategies for Teaching Grammar

1. Develop awareness
- Ask questions that help students become aware of the form of the structure. For example, for *yes / no* questions in the present progressive (FOG 1, page 117, Grammar Notes 1–2), make a statement, "You are working," and select a student to form the corresponding question. *(Are you working?)* Ask what verb form is used in the statement and question. *(present progressive)* Select another student to give a short answer to the question. *(Yes, I am* OR *No, I'm not.)* Ask what verb form is used in that answer. *(simple present)* Continue with other statements, questions, and answers, selecting new students each time.
- Compare information in the Grammar Charts. For example, the comparison of simple past *wh-* questions about the subject and those that are not about the subject (FOG 1, page 179) shows a difference in the use of *did* in questions and in answers. Ask, "What verb do we need to add in order to make a simple past *wh-* question that is not about the subject?" *(did)* Then ask, "Do we need to add a verb for questions about the subject? *(no)* Finally, ask, "When can we use *did* in answers to simple past *wh-* questions? *(in answers to questions about the subject)*

2. Present meaning
Show the meaning of a grammatical form through a classroom demonstration. For example, to illustrate the use of the present progressive, you could show pictures of actions in the process of happening: a picture of a person in a supermarket pushing a shopping cart *(He / She is shopping)*; a picture of two people playing tennis or Ping-Pong *(They are playing tennis / Ping-Pong)*; or a picture of a person dining at a restaurant *(He / She is eating.)*.

3. Identify examples
Ask students to go back to the Grammar in Context section and label examples in the reading passage with the grammatical terms in the Grammar Charts.

4. Generate examples
Find examples from the reading or elsewhere that could fit into the Grammar Charts. An interesting way to do this is to photocopy and enlarge the Grammar Chart. White out the targeted structures and replace them with blank lines for each missing word. Make copies and distribute them to students in pairs or small groups. Have students fill in the blanks, using examples from the reading. Then generate more examples. Books can be open or closed, depending on the level of challenge desired.

5. Show understanding by categorizing
Check comprehension of a grammatical principle by asking students to label multiple examples appropriately. For example, students can label verbs "present" or "future" or they can label examples "correct" or "incorrect."

6. Show understanding by performing actions
Check comprehension of the meaning of a grammatical form by having students follow instructions. Ask students, for example, to think of and perform a set of actions that they could describe using the present progressive.

7. Manipulate forms
Have students manipulate the examples in the Grammar Charts to practice the form. Drills such as substitution or transformation help students to build fluency. For example, in Unit 31 (FOG 1, page 244), you might have students look at examples in Notes 1–3 and change the affirmative statements to negative ones, or vice versa. Then, working from either affirmative or negative statements, have students add future time expressions.

8. Personalize
Ask students to provide personal examples. For example, on page 229 in Exercise 2, students read about the nicest people encountered by some travelers in Scotland. Have two or three students, in turn, share with the rest of the class a story about the nicest people they have met while traveling. For example:

S1: The nicest people I met were some Italians. They showed us a great restaurant in Rome.

S2: The nicest people I met were some Egyptians. They helped me when I was lost.

9. Repeat, reinforce

Students need to be exposed to new grammar many times in order to internalize it completely. You can first present a new structure on the board, then point it out in the book, then have students use it in an informal oral exercise, then do a written exercise in pairs, and finally review the same structure in homework. Varying the content and focus of these activities will keep students interested, and the grammar will be reinforced almost automatically.

Frequently Asked Questions (FAQ)

1. When should I have students work in pairs or groups rather than individually or as a whole class?

Varying your classroom organization to suit particular activity types will result in more effective and more interesting classes. Many students are not accustomed to working in pairs or groups, so it is important to use these groupings only when they are most beneficial.

- **Whole-class teaching** maximizes teacher control and is especially good for:
  - —presenting information, giving explanations and instructions
  - —showing material in texts and pictures or on audio or videotape
  - —teacher-led drills (such as substitution or transformation) or dictations
  - —reviewing answers or sharing ideas after students have completed an activity
  - —enabling the whole class to benefit from teacher feedback to individuals
- **Students working individually** allows quiet, concentrated attention and is most effective for:
  - —processing information or completing a task at students' own pace
  - —performing writing tasks

For objective exercises such as fill-in-the-blank, matching, multiple choice, and editing, vary your class organization to keep student motivation high. Students can sometimes complete these exercises individually, and sometimes they can work with a partner.

- **Students working in pairs** maximizes student speaking time, breaks up the routine and "teacher talk," and is ideal for:
  - —information-gap activities
  - —role plays
  - —writing and/or reading dialogues
  - —predicting the content of reading and listening texts
  - —comparing notes on what students listen to or see
  - —checking answers
  - —peer assessment

Pair work can also be very effective for completing objective exercises such as fill-in-the-blank, matching, multiple choice, and editing.

- **Students working in groups** creates ideal conditions for students to learn from each other and works well for:
  - —generating ideas
  - —pooling knowledge
  - —writing group stories
  - —preparing presentations
  - —discussing an issue and reaching a group decision

2. How should I set up pair work and group work?

- **Streaming:** Grouping students according to ability or participation has certain advantages.
  - **ability:** Grouping weaker and stronger students together allows more able students to help their less fluent classmates.
  - **participation:** If you see that some students participate less than others, you could make a pair or group of weak participators. By the same token, you can also put especially talkative students together.
- **Chance:** Grouping students by chance has many benefits, especially if it results in students working with varied partners. You can group students by chance according to:
  - **where they sit:** Students sitting next to or near one another work in pairs or groups. This is the easiest option, but if students always sit in the same place, you will want to find other ways of grouping them.
  - **the "wheels" system:** Half the class stands in a circle facing outward, and the other half stands in an outer circle facing inward. The outer circle revolves in a clockwise direction, and the inner circle revolves in a counterclockwise direction. When you tell them to stop, students work with the person facing them. This is a very effective way to have students engage in meaningful repetition, such as asking the same question of many different partners.
  - **assigned letters:** Assign each student a letter from *A* to *E*. Then ask all the As to form a group, all the Bs to form a group, and so on.
  - **birthdays:** Students stand in a line in the order of their birthdays (with January at one end and December at the other). The first five students form one group; the second five students another group; and so on.
  - **native language:** If possible, put students in groups or pairs with others who don't

share a native language. This helps create an "English only" classroom.

3. How can I make activities more successful?

Before the activity:

- **Motivate students and explain the purpose.** Make it clear that something enjoyable or interesting is going to happen. Explain the rationale for the activity. By making sure students understand the purpose of the activity is to practice what they learned, you will encourage them to participate more.
- **Provide clear directions.** Explain what students should do in every step of the activity. Have students paraphrase or demonstrate the task to be sure they understand it.
- **Demonstrate.** Show the class what is supposed to happen in an activity. This might involve asking a student to demonstrate the activity with you or having two students role-play in the front of the room.
- **Provide a time frame.** It is helpful for students to know how much time they have and exactly when they should stop. Approximate times are given for all the activities in this Teacher's Manual.

For open-ended activities you will also want to:

- **Stimulate thinking.** Where there are choices for students to make, it is often helpful to set up small-group and/or whole-class brainstorming sessions to define the focus and/or content of their task.
- **Prepare language.** Review grammar and vocabulary that students may need to complete the task. This can be done as a follow-up to a brainstorming activity where you elicit ideas and write key language on the board.

During the activity:

- **Observe students.** Walk around the room watching and listening to pairs or groups.
- **Provide assistance as needed.** (See FAQ 5 for suggestions on giving feedback and correcting errors.)

After the activity:

- **Elicit student responses.** For some activities you may ask for volunteers or call on students to share some of their ideas with the class. For other types of activities, a few pairs or groups can be asked to role-play their discussions to demonstrate the language they have been using.

- **Provide feedback.** In many cases, this is most conveniently done in a whole-class setting. It may be preferable, however, for you to meet with individuals, pairs, or groups. While the principal focus in a grammar class is language use, it is also important to acknowledge the value of students' ideas. See FAQ 5 for suggestions on feedback and error correction.

4. What can I do to encourage students to use more English in the classroom?

It is perfectly natural for students to feel the need to use their first language in an English class. There are a number of actions that teachers can take to promote the use of English.

- **Set clear guidelines.** Indicate when it will be acceptable to use students' native language. For example, some teachers in monolingual classes find that activities such as providing vocabulary definitions, presenting a grammar point, checking comprehension, giving instructions, and discussing classroom methodology are best done in the students' native language.
- **Use persuasion.** Walking among the students during speaking activities and saying things like, "Please speak English!" or "Try to use English as much as possible" helps to ensure that most students will speak English most of the time.

5. What's the best approach to giving feedback and correcting errors?

Be selective in offering correction. Students can't focus on everything at once, so concentrate first on errors relating to the target grammar point and grammar points from units previously studied, as well as any errors that interfere with communication. Whether you respond to other errors depends on your judgment of students' readiness to take in the information. If you see a teachable moment, seize it! Rather than correct every error individual students make in the course of activities, it is generally preferable to note commonly occurring mistakes and give a short presentation for the whole class at the end of the activity.

- **Recasting.** If a student makes an error—for example, "I *didn't came* to class yesterday because I was sick."—you can recast it as, "You *didn't come* to class yesterday because you were sick?" The student ideally notices the difference and restates the original sentence: "Right. I didn't come to class yesterday because I was sick." This process can be effective because the student has the opportunity to self-correct an error that is still in short-term memory. As a variation, you can restate but stop, with rising intonation, right before the potential error: "You didn't . . . ?"

6. What can I do to accommodate different learning styles?

Focus on Grammar recognizes different styles of learning and provides a variety of activities to accommodate these different styles. Some learners prefer an analytical, or rule-learning (deductive), approach. Others, especially younger learners, respond best to an inductive approach, or exposure to the language in meaningful contexts. Indeed, the same students may adopt different styles as they learn or may use different styles at different times.

As teachers, we want to help the students in our classes who prefer to follow rules become more able to take risks and to plunge into communicative activities. We also want to encourage the risk-takers to focus on accuracy. *Focus on Grammar* provides the variety to ensure that students achieve their goal: to learn to use the language confidently and appropriately.

Unit-by-Unit Teaching Tips

Unit Overview

In Unit 1 students will learn affirmative and negative forms of the imperative.

Grammar in Context (pages 2–3)

Comprehension Questions

• Who is driving? *(Mark)*
• Who is giving directions? *(Steve)*
• Where are the men going? *(to a restaurant)*
• Where is the gas station? *(on Jackson Street)*
• Where is the restaurant? *(on Third Avenue)*
• Where do the men park? *(behind a truck)*
• What does the sign on the door say? *(Closed for vacation)*

Grammar Presentation (page 4)

Identify the Grammar

AFFIRMATIVE	NEGATIVE
<u>Drive</u> to the corner.	<u>Don't worry</u>.
<u>Turn</u> left.	<u>Don't park</u> here.

Grammar Charts

• Write the examples of the target grammar from the reading on the board. Underline the imperatives. Read the sentences out loud and have students repeat. Pantomime the actions of the verbs.
• Read, pantomime, and have students repeat the language in the chart. Ask:
  —What are imperatives? *(commands, verbs)*
  —Which words are imperatives? *(turn, park, don't turn, don't park)*
  —In affirmative imperatives, which word is first? *(a verb)*

—In negative imperatives, which word is first? *(don't)*

Grammar Notes

Note 1 *(Exercises 2–5)*
• Make a chart like the following on the board or an overhead transparency:

Directions	Instructions	Requests

• Call students up to the board. Tell them to write additional affirmative and negative examples of each type of imperative as you say them. Choose imperatives that students can carry out. Choose students to act out the examples. For example:
  —Directions: Carlos, go to the window.
  —Instructions: Use basic commands, e.g., *Stand up, Sit down, Don't talk.*
  —Requests: Tekun, please close your book. Hannah and Miko, please don't talk now.
• Put students in pairs. Tell each pair to write two additional examples of each type of imperative. Circulate as they write. Select students to add their examples to the chart. Call on other students to read the new examples and say if they are correct.

Note 2 *(Exercises 2–5)*
Write a set of five or six sentences on the board. Some should have errors. Call on students to read each sentence and say if it is correct or incorrect. If it is incorrect, have students correct it. For example:
• *You sit down.*
• *Opens the window.*
• *Come here.*
• *Stand up.*
• *Turning left.*

Note 3 *(Exercises 2–5)*

Do a quick drill using the imperatives already on the board. Have the class change them to negatives. For example:

T: Turn off the light.

CLASS: Don't turn off the light.

Note 4 *(Exercises 3–5)*

Once again, use the verbs and phrases on the board to perform a quick drill. Point to a phrase and have the class restate it using *please*.

→ For additional practice, see the Supplementary Activities on page 89.

Focused Practice *(pages 4–7)*

Exercise 4

Demonstrate *circle, underline, change*.

driveway: a short road that leads to one house only

garage: a place where a car, bus, etc., is kept

Exercise 5

broken: in pieces because of being hit, dropped, etc.

Exercise 6

complete: to finish doing or making something

Communication Practice *(pages 7–8)*

Exercise 7

- Before listening, say the numbers and have students repeat. Then say the numbers in random order and have students hold up fingers to show comprehension. Finally, have individual students say the numbers and their classmates respond with fingers.
- Have students read the items in the exercise and predict words that could fit in the blanks. Confirm answers that could be correct, e.g.:

  S: "Study the words on page 10."

  T: Yes, that is possible.

- After listening, have students work in pairs and compare answers. Then have them take turns reading the passage out loud.

Exercise 8

- Read the items in the box and have students repeat. For verbs, have students pantomime the action. For nouns, write your name, e-mail address, etc., on the board and have students identify the body parts. For other nouns, have students point to an example.

- Model the activity. Call up one student and make a request. The student should comply. Then switch roles.
- Next, call up two students in front of the class to do the same.
- Have students work in pairs. Circulate and monitor to make sure listeners are doing or pantomiming the request they hear.

Exercise 9

- This exercise may be confusing, so model it first with a student. For Part A, have the student read the directions. Hold up the book and let the class see you tracing the route based on the directions you hear. At the end of the directions, ask the class: "Where am I?" They should respond *(at Westlake Park)*. Check answer "a."
- For Part B, give directions and have the class trace the route. Make sure students understand that they should start at Union and 3rd Avenue. For example: "You are at Union Street and 3rd Avenue. Walk five blocks to 3rd Avenue and Lenora. Turn left and go three blocks. Where are you?" *(Victor Steinbrueck Park)*
- Provide further practice by giving a different starting point, e.g., 8th and Pike.

Further Practice

Play a version of "Mother, May I?" In this popular children's game, a speaker gives a command. Listeners must say "Mother, may I?" before carrying out the command. If the speaker says "Yes, you may," listeners perform the action. If the speaker says "No, you may not," listeners should do nothing. If a listener performs the command without saying "Mother, may I?" the person is "out."

Preparation

Make and distribute a handout of basic commands, or use other commands you want your students to learn. For example:

stand up	sneeze	whisper
sit down	giggle	hum
touch the (floor)	stand on one foot	hop
raise your (leg)	flex your	shout
scratch your	muscles	stretch
(nose)	shrug your	yawn
turn your head	shoulders	sing
drum your	wave	make a fist
fingers	tickle (someone)	turn on / off
blow a kiss	clap	(the light)
cough	cry	

Say and demonstrate each command. Have students repeat. Do a comprehension check: Say a command and check that students respond appropriately. Have students quiz each other in pairs.

Play the Game
Students should stand up and face forward. Model a few rounds of the game. Say a command and wait for students to say "Mother, may I?" Respond "Yes, you may" or "No, you may not" and check that students respond appropriately. Select students in turn to come up before the class and issue commands.

 OUT OF THE BOX ......

Imperative treasure hunt. The purpose of this activity is to enable students to find authentic uses of the imperative. Collect English-language newspapers or magazines, enough for every three or four students in your class. Put students in small groups. Give them a blank chart like the one in Grammar Notes, Note 1. Instruct them to leaf through newspapers or their magazines and record examples of directions, instructions, and requests that use the imperative. Give a time limit. When time is up, call a representative of each group to come before the class and demonstrate the group's findings.

If you are in an English-speaking country, you can vary this activity by putting students in teams and instructing them to go into the community and find examples of imperatives on signs, billboards, and posters. (Typical examples: *Walk / Don't walk*) If students have camera phones or digital cameras, they can even take pictures of the examples they encounter.

UNIT 2 *This is / These are; Subject Pronouns*

Unit Overview

In Unit 2 students will learn the use of *This is, These are,* and subject pronouns in statements and questions.

Grammar in Context (pages 9–10)

Comprehension Questions
- Where is Steve's apartment? *(in Seattle)*
- Who is Pam? *(a parrot)*
- Who is Kip? *(a cat)*
- Who is Jessica? *(Steve's sister)*

Words
To further illustrate the words, show the class pictures of your family or another family you know. After modeling, hold up the pictures and elicit the target vocabulary from the students.

Expressions
- Walk around the room and model Conversation 1 with two or three students. Then have students turn to people sitting near them and practice.
- Call up two students and model Conversation 2 with them. Then number students off in groups of three to practice.
- Model Conversation 3 for the class. Alternate saying the first and second lines.
- Have students stand up, walk around, and make introductions using all the expressions. Once they have introduced themselves to someone, they can then introduce that person to a third student.

Working Together
Part A
Have two students take turns reading the sentences from the opening reading out loud. Correct pronunciation as needed. Then have students read in pairs.

Grammar Presentation (pages 11–12)

Identify the Grammar

This is my apartment in Seattle.
It's small but comfortable.
These are my pets.
They're wonderful.

Grammar Charts
- Write the examples of the target grammar from the reading on the board. Underline the target structures.
- Ask questions to help students notice the grammar. Point to the underlined items on the board and the corresponding pictures in the student text as you read the example sentences. Have students repeat. Introduce

the terms *singular, plural, subject pronouns, contractions,* e.g.:
—This is Steve's apartment. How many apartments? *(one)*
—What is *this*? *(Steve's apartment)*
—Is *this* singular or plural? *(singular)*
—It's small. What is *it*? *(Steve's apartment)*
—What is *'s*? *(It's a contraction.)*
—Is *it* singular or plural? *(singular)*
—What is *it's*? *(a contraction of it is)*

• Ask similar questions to introduce the plural forms.

• Read and have students repeat the forms and examples in the charts. Use gestures to illustrate the sentences, and form similar true sentences with the names of your students and objects in your classroom, e.g.:
—This is my student Katja. She's from Poland.
—This is my desk. It's messy.

Grammar Notes

Notes 1–2 *(Exercise 2)*
• Walk around the room and make sentences with *This is* and *These are*. Point out both objects and people, e.g.: *This is Paula. These are Jorge and Ahmed. This is a stapler. These are my books.*

• Continue walking around the room. Point but do not speak. Have students form the sentences. If students do not know the name of an item you point to, prompt them by pointing and saying only the name, e.g., *scissors.*

Note 3 *(Exercise 2)*
• Do a fast transformation drill. Say sentences with *this* and *these*. Students should respond with the question form. For example:

T: This is a grammar book.

CLASS: Is this a grammar book?

T: These are old shoes.

CLASS: Are these old shoes?

• Have students form both questions and answers. Provide noun clues. Point to the speakers. For example:

T: a cheese sandwich

S1: This is a cheese sandwich.

S2: Is this a cheese sandwich?

T: my glasses

S1: These are my glasses.

S2: Are these my (your) glasses?

• Now make the activity more meaningful. Walk around the room and have each student put a personal object in a bag. (Make sure there are some plural objects, such as glasses or keys.) Make sure the class does not see what each student puts in. When you have collected objects from everyone, call on students in turn to come up before the class, reach into the bag, select an item, and try to locate its owner as follows:

S1: Marta, is this your lipstick?

MARTA: Yes, it is. [S1 returns lipstick to Marta.]

S2: Makiko, are these your keys?

MAKIKO: No, they aren't / they're not.

S2: Kirithorn, are these your keys?

KIRITHORN: Yes, they are. [S2 returns keys.]

• This activity can also be done in groups.

Note 4 *(Exercises 2–3)*
• On the board, write examples of words that take an *-es* ending. Say the singular and plural forms and have students repeat. For example:

class	classes
watch	watches
box	boxes
dish	dishes

• Write a list of singular nouns on the board. Include nouns whose plural forms end in both *-s* and *-es*. Call students up to the board to write the plurals. Examples: *dog, sandwich, cross, book, fox, wish, room.*

Note 5 *(Exercises 2–3)*
• On the board or a transparency, make a chart like the one below, but leave blanks. Elicit the missing forms from the students and fill in the chart yourself, or have a student write them in.

Subject Pronoun	Verb	Contraction
I	am	I'm
you	are	
		he's
she		
it		
		we're
they		

- Use pictures of your family or your friends, or bring in magazine pictures of famous people. Make sentences with *this is* and *these are* + noun objects. Point to students, and have them follow up with a sentence beginning with a contracted form. For example:

T: This is my cousin Judy.

S1: She's pretty.

T: And this is my husband.

S2: He's handsome.

T: These are my cats.

S3: They're cute.

Focused Practice (pages 12–13)

Exercise 3

roommate: someone who shares a room or house with someone else

parents: mother and father

journalism: the job of writing for a newspaper, magazine, television, or radio

Communication Practice (page 14)

Exercise 5

- For Part B, extend the exercise as follows: S1 closes his or her book. S2, with book open, says one of the sentences. S1 responds from memory with the other sentence. Students switch roles after four or five sentences.
- Circulate as students are talking and help as needed.

Exercise 6

- Before students begin working in groups, model the activity with a student. Be sure to model both the question and statement forms.
- Call up two students to model the activity again. Correct errors and provide direction as needed.
- As students work in groups, circulate and help with grammar and pronunciation.

Exercise 7

Bring in additional objects and teach their names using *This is* and *These are*. Kitchen objects will work well. Next, "plant" the objects around the room. Carry out the activity according to the directions in the book.

Exercise 8

Photos from popular magazines such as *People* will also work well for this activity.

Further Practice

Have students draw a diagram of their house, apartment, or room. Encourage them to add details such as plants, trophies, paintings on the wall, etc. Put students in small groups. Instruct students to share their diagrams and talk about them using statements and questions with *This is* and *These are*. For example:

S1: This is my apartment. It's very small.

S2: Is this your bedroom?

S1: No, it's the kitchen. This is the bedroom.

Map activity. Go to a teachers' resource website and find a map of a continent that your students are not well acquainted with. Print out the map and erase the names of the countries. At the top or on the back, add a word box containing the names of all the countries you erased. Then make enough copies of this handout for every two or three students. Put students in small groups. Instruct them to work together, using the language from this unit, to write in the names of the countries. Model a sample exchange such as the following:

S1: This is Mali.

S2: OK. Is this Sierra Leone?

S3: No, it's not. It's Ghana.

If you wish to make this a competitive activity, then the first group to fill out the map correctly is the winner.

The Present of *Be*: Statements

Unit Overview

In Unit 3 students will learn the forms of *be* in present affirmative and negative statements.

Grammar in Context (pages 18–19)

Background Notes

- The capital of Australia is Canberra. Sydney is the largest city.
- Seattle is in the state of Washington. It is the state's most famous city, but it is not the capital; the capital is Olympia.

Comprehension Questions

- Is Amy a woman or a man? *(a woman)*
- Are Amy and Jenny on vacation? *(Yes, they are.)*
- Are Amy and Jenny from Seattle? *(No, they're from Australia.)*
- Is Seattle dirty? *(No, it's clean.)*

Words and Expressions

- Have students name things that are clean, dirty, delicious, or awful.
- Model the expressions with a student. Personalize the first dialogue by telling where you are really from. Finally, have students practice the conversations in pairs. Remind them to respond truthfully to the first question.

Working Together

- For Part A, circulate as students practice the conversation.
- Call up three students to perform the conversation in front of the class.
- For Part B, model and have students repeat the answers.
- For Part C, model the conversation with a student. Then circulate as students practice in pairs. Take note of errors and go over them after the class has finished practicing.
- Extend the activity by having students make truthful sentences about the city they are in. Encourage them to use negative sentences and other adjectives they know, for example:
  —The people are not friendly.
  —The city is dirty.
  —The food is awful.

Grammar Presentation (pages 20–21)

Identify the Grammar

AFFIRMATIVE
I *am* (from Seattle).
It*'s* a wonderful city.
We*'re* from Australia.
They*'re* here on vacation.

NEGATIVE
You*'re not* from around here.

Grammar Charts

- Ask questions to help students notice the grammar. Point to the items in the charts and ask questions such as the following:
  —*It's* is a contraction. What is the long form? *(It is)*
  —*We're* is also a contraction. What is the long form? *(We are)*
  —What are the three affirmative forms of the be verb? *(am, is, are)*
  —Which word do we use to make a negative verb? *(not)*
  —Where do we put it? *(after am, is, are)*
- Do a series of quick matching and transformation drills with pronouns and verbs. Continue until students are able to match subjects and verbs easily, for example:
Affirmative

T: I	Ss: am
T: You	Ss: are

Negative

T: We	S1: We're not	S2: We aren't

Grammar Notes

Notes 1 and 2 *(Exercises 2–6)*
Do a quick transformation drill. Say an affirmative sentence. The class should change it to the negative. Be sure to include all three forms of the *be* verb, e.g.:

T: I am from New York.	Ss: I am not from New York.
T: It is hot today.	Ss: It is not hot today.
T: We are happy.	Ss: We are not happy.

Note 3 *(Exercises 4–5)*

• Some students may benefit from a visual representation of the information in this note. Draw the following on the board:

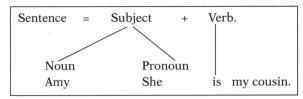

• Say or point to similar sentences already on the board and elicit the sentence parts from the students.

Note 4 *(Exercises 4–5)*

Have students summarize the forms by filling in a chart like the one below.

Pronoun	Affirmative	Contraction	Negative	Contraction(s)
I	I am	I'm	I am not	I'm not
You				
He				
She				
It				
We				
They				

Focused Practice (pages 21–23)

Exercise 4
youth hostel: an inexpensive hotel for young people

Exercise 5
fine: very well

Communication Practice (page 24)

Exercise 7
As a follow-up, give students copies of the script and have them practice the conversation in pairs. Next, have them substitute real information about themselves for the names and places in the conversation. Finally, have them practice the conversation without looking at the script.

Exercise 8
• Extend Part B by having students correct the false statements.
• If your class is large, have students do Part B in pairs or small groups.

Further Practice
Have students prepare a 30-second speech using the language from this unit. Instruct them to use contractions, for example:

I'm Tina, and I'm from Kiev. Kiev is the capital of Ukraine. It's a big, old, and very beautiful city, but it's very polluted from the Chernobyl accident. I'm a student here, but in Kiev I'm a dentist. My mother and father are in Kiev too. My father is 78 years old and he's retired. My mother is a housewife.

Give students time to write their speeches in class. Circulate and help with needed vocabulary. Have students practice their speeches in pairs. Partners should monitor each other's speech for agreement of subject and verb and proper use of contractions. Call students up one by one to speak before the class. After each student finishes speaking, encourage the class to ask follow-up questions. Examples: *Is your mother young? Is Kiev hot? Is it noisy?*

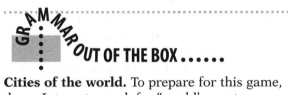

GRAMMAR OUT OF THE BOX......

Cities of the world. To prepare for this game, do an Internet search for "world's most populous cities." Prepare a handout with a list of the cities. Also, write the name of each city on an index card. Prepare enough cards for every one or two students in your class. Distribute the cards and instruct students not to tell anyone which city they got. For homework, have students answer the following questions about "their" cities; they may use the unit vocabulary in parentheses or choose their own words.

Which country is your city in? _____
Is it the capital? _____
How is the weather? (hot, cold, cool, warm) _____
_____
How is the city? (new, old, expensive, beautiful, clean, dirty, noisy, crowded)_____
How are the people? (friendly, not friendly) _____
_____
How is the food? (delicious, awful)_____

Back in class, hand out the list of cities to everyone. Call students up in front of the class to tell about their cities. The class then guesses which city it is. For example:

S1: My city is in the United States. It is not the capital. The weather is cold in the winter, hot in the summer. It's expensive, noisy, and crowded, but also very wonderful. The people are not friendly. They are very busy. The food is great.

Ss: Is it New York?

S1: Yes, it is.

UNIT 4
That is / Those are; Possessive Adjectives; Plural Nouns

Unit Overview

In Unit 4 students will learn the use of *That is, Those are,* possessive adjectives, and plural nouns.

Grammar in Context (pages 25–26)

Background Notes

- Paul Allen co-founded Microsoft Corporation with Bill Gates in 1975. He is one of the richest people in the world.
- A person's "baby," used in this context, is the person's favorite project or hobby.

Comprehension Questions

- Is Jenny with Steve and Amy? *(no)*
- What are the big buildings? *(stadiums)*
- What does Amy look through? *(binoculars)*
- What is the colored building? *(the EMP)*
- What is the EMP? *(a music museum)*

Words and Expressions

- As a follow-up to learning the words and practicing their pronunciation, do a spelling test.
- Create a gapped version of the dialogues in the Expressions box. Have students fill in the gaps with other words they know, for example:

A: How about a _____?

B: That's a _____ idea.

A: It's too bad _____ isn't here.

B: Yeah.

A: That's your _____, right?

B: _____.

Working Together

Follow up by creating a similar riddle about a landmark in the city where you are.

Grammar Presentation (pages 27–28)

Identify the Grammar

Is that it?
That's the Space Needle.
What *are those* big *buildings*?
And *those are people* next to them.
That's your university, right?
Its shape is really unusual.

Grammar Charts

- Ask questions to help students notice the grammar, for example:
  —Are the words *that, those,* and *people* singular or plural? *(singular, plural, plural, respectively)*
  —What is the subject of "Is that your key?" What is the verb? *(that, is)*
  —What is the subject of "Its shape is unusual?" What is the verb? *(shape, is)*
  —What are the words *your* and *its*? *(possessive adjectives)*
- Call on students to read the sentences in the first chart. Follow up by illustrating the contrast between *this / that* and *these / those.* Place a few objects near you and similar objects a short distance away. Be sure to include plural items such as glasses, keys, headphones, or scissors. Demonstrate the contrasts by speaking and pointing, e.g.:
  —This is my wallet. That's Amir's wallet.
  —These are my keys. Those are Sarah's keys.
- Next, call on students to form the sentences as you point.
- Call on students to read the items in the second chart.
- Do a few quick drills. Say the possessive adjective. Have students respond with the subject pronoun. Afterward reverse the order, e.g.:

T: its   Ss: it

T: they   Ss: their

- For the third chart, say the singular and try to elicit the plurals from the class. Write the unfamiliar forms, such as *people*, on the board, e.g.:

  T: girl   Ss: girls

  T: person   Ss: people

- Model the pronunciation of the singular-plural pairs, e.g., *man / men, woman / women*, etc.
- Drill. Say one form. The class says the other. Example:

  T: child   Ss: children

Grammar Notes

Notes 1 and 2 *(Exercises 2–3)*

Make an overhead transparency from a map or a diagram with singular and plural locations visible. A neighborhood or campus map or a diagram of a room or garden will work well. Have students come up to the projector, point to an item, and ask, *What's that?* or *What are those?* Answer the questions with *That's (a / my)* _____ or *Those are (my)* _____*s*. Here are some examples:

S: What's that?

T: That's a park. It's about five minutes from my house.

S: What are those?

T: Those are tennis courts.

S: What are those (plants)?

T: Those are roses. And this is a sunflower.

Notes 3 and 4 *(Exercises 2–4)*

- Do a fast transformation drill. Say a statement. Students change it to a question. Here are some examples:

  T: That's my watch.   Ss: Is that your watch?

  T: Those are my scissors?   Ss: Are those your scissors?

- Bring in photos of yourself with groups of people, or use magazine photos of groups of people. (It is amusing to students if you show them a picture of you as a child or teenager.) Use one photo to model sentences using possessive adjectives, e.g.:

  This is me at age 14. That's my sister Joyce, and that's her boyfriend. This is my mother, and this is her brother, my uncle

George. That's his dog. I can't remember its name. My father isn't in this picture.

- Elicit questions from the students about the people and things in another picture; answer truthfully. For example:

  S1: Is that your car?

  T: No, it's my father's car.

  S2: Is it expensive?

  T: Yes, it's a 1965 Mustang. It's a classic.

- Put students in pairs or small groups and have them follow your example with photos of them with their families or friends.
- On the board, a handout, or a transparency, prepare an exercise to help students learn the different spellings of the items that sound alike, for example:

  Mother to child: I am not happy with you. (Your / you're) _____ *late, and (your / you're)* _____ *dirty clothes are on the floor. Please clean up (your / you're)* _____ *room. Put your shoes in (their / they're)* _____ *boxes. (Their / They're)* _____ *dirty.*

→ For additional practice, see the Supplementary Activities on page 89.

Note 5 *(Exercises 3–4)*

Repeat or review the activity for Unit 2, Note 4, page 18.

Focused Practice *(pages 29–31)*

Exercise 2

wallet: a small flat case for cards or paper money, usually carried in a pocket or purse

Exercise 3

belongs: is owned by someone

battery: an object that provides electricity for a radio, car, etc.

dead: (of a battery) not working

run: (of an object such as a car) to work or be working

favorite: liked more than others

Exercise 4

purse: a bag used by women to carry money and personal things

turn: the time when it is a person's chance or duty to do something

Exercise 5

tire: a thick round piece of rubber that fits around the wheel of a car, bicycle, etc.

flat: a tire that is flat does not have enough air in it

Communication Practice (page 31)

Exercise 6

Have students read the conversation in pairs.

Exercise 7

A humorous variation of this activity is to collect students' lunches (or cell phones) and follow the same procedure.

Further Practice

Put students in pairs or small groups. Give each group a list of four or five words from this chapter, including at least one irregular plural, for example:

| cats | dog | huge | their | women |

Tell students to make up short stories using all the words in their list. They can add as many words and details as they want, for example:

> *This is my dog. His name is Brutus. He's huge. These are my cats. Their names are Bonnie and Clyde. Brutus likes my cats. He always eats their food, so they don't like him!*

Have one student from each group tell the group's story to the class. Follow up by using the students' stories for dictation practice.

GRAMMAR OUT OF THE BOX ......

Vacation photos. Have students bring in photographs of a vacation or special occasion. Divide the class into two groups. The students in one group remain seated and prepare a display of their photos at their desks. The other students walk around and "visit" the photo displays. They ask questions about the people, things, and places using *this, that, these, those*. The seated students answer using possessive pronouns and other words as appropriate. At a signal from the teacher, the groups switch.

The Present of *Be:* Yes / *No* Questions, Questions with *Who* and *What*

UNIT 5

Unit Overview

In Unit 5 students will learn how to ask and answer *yes / no* questions with *be* and information questions with *who* and *what*.

Grammar in Context (pages 32–33)

Comprehension Questions

- Who is Steve? *(Amanda's cousin)*
- Who is Mark? *(Josh's friend)*
- Is Mark married? *(No, he's not.)*
- Who is with Amanda? *(Kathy)*

Words and Expressions

- To further illustrate the words, ask the class who is married and who is single.
- To practice the expressions, have students stand up, circulate, and ask authentic questions using *What about you* and *What do you do*, for example:

T: I'm 31 years old. What about you?

S: I'm 18.

T: What do you do?

S: I'm a student.

Working Together

Part A
Call up four students to read and act out the conversations in front of the class. Then have students read the conversations in pairs.

Part B
Extend the list to include the professions or future occupations of your students, e.g., a housewife, a businessman, etc. Have students state their occupations in a chain as follows:

T: I'm a teacher. How about you, Carmen?

CARMEN: I'm a dancer. How about you, Tomoki?

Part C
Have students get up and circulate again. At a signal from you, such as a hand clap, students should "freeze" and pair up with the person nearest them. The two should then follow the example in the text to talk about another pair of students. Repeat several times until students can conduct the conversation without reading.

Grammar Presentation (pages 34–35)

Identify the Grammar

Are you here for the wedding? *Yes, I am.*
Who's that man with Steve?
Is he single? *Yes, he is.*
Is she married? *No, she's not.*

Grammar Charts

- Write the examples of the target grammar from the reading on the board.
- Write a statement on the board, e.g., *We are here for the wedding.* Ask the students:
  —Which word is first in a statement? *(the subject)*
  —Which word is second? *(the verb)*
- Point to the *yes / no* questions on the board. Focus students' attention on the question mark. Ask:
  —Which word is first in this question? *(the verb)*
  —Which word is second? *(the subject)*
  —What is the answer to these questions? *(yes or no)*
- Point to the questions with *who* and *what*. Ask:
  —Which word comes after *who* and *what*? *(the verb)*
- Elicit answers to the questions with *who* and *what*, for example:

  T: Who's that man with Steve?

  S1: His name is Mark. / That's Mark.

  T: What does he do?

  S2: He's a writer / a student, etc.
- Draw students' attention to the different intonation patterns of *yes / no* and information questions. Use your hand to show rising and falling intonation as you say the questions. Have students repeat after you and gesture to show the intonation pattern.

Grammar Notes

Note 1 *(Exercises 2, 4–5)*
Do a transformation drill. Say a statement. Have students change it to a question. Here are some examples:

T: I am late.	Ss: Am I late?
T: You are tired.	Ss: Are you tired?

Note 2 *(Exercises 2, 4–5)*
- Do a series of drills to reinforce answers with contractions. Ask questions with a variety of subjects.
- Examples of questions with *yes* answers (no contractions):
  —Are you a student? *(Yes, I am.)*
  —Is today (Tuesday)? *(Yes, it is.)*
  —Are we in room 20? *(Yes, we are.)*
- Examples of questions with *no* answers; instruct students to use contracted forms:
  —Are you a doctor? *(No, I'm not.)*
  —Is today (Friday)? *(No, it isn't. / No, it's not.)*
  —Are we Japanese? *(No, we're not. / No, we aren't.)*
- Ask questions that take *yes* or *no* answers and instruct students to answer truthfully, e.g.:
  —Do you like cats?
  —Are Americans friendly?
  —Is my English easy to understand?

Note 3 *(Exercises 3–5)*
- If your class is large and students do not yet know each other, use the example questions to help students learn each other's names. Have a student point to someone he or she does not know and ask, *Who's that?* or *What's her name?* The class responds with the name.
- If students know each other's names, bring in various denominations of American money. Show each bill, point to the picture on the back, and ask, *Who's that? What's his name?* For example, a $20 bill has a picture of Andrew Jackson on it.

Focused Practice (pages 35–37)

Exercise 1

cousin: the child of your aunt or uncle

actually: a word used to show that you are giving real or true information about something

Communication Practice (pages 37–38)

Exercise 7

Have students correct their answers in pairs. One student reads the question. The other reads answers. Then they switch.

Exercise 8
Part A
- Pass around straight pins or tape. Have each student write the name of a famous person on a card. Then have students pin or tape

their paper to the back of the person sitting in front of them.
- Magazine photos can be used instead of the cards.

Part B

Elicit questions students could ask using words they know and write the questions on the board. For example:
- *Am I tall / rich / nice / married?*
- *Am I a singer / an actor?*
- *Am I American / English / Taiwanese?*

Further Practice

Play a game of "20 Questions." This game is similar to the one in Exercise 8. Write the names of famous people on slips of paper and put all the slips into a hat or box. Call students up one by one to draw a name out of the hat. The class asks *yes / no* questions beginning with *Are you . . . ?* They must try to guess who the person is in 20 questions or fewer. Sample questions:
- Are you a man?
- Are you American?
- Are you famous in Korea?
- Are you old?
- Are you a singer?
- Is your hair black?
- Is your music noisy?

OUT OF THE BOX . . . . . .

Interview. Have students interview a person outside of your class or school. Have students write five or more questions to ask, for example:
- What's your name?
- What do you do?
- Is your job interesting?
- Are you happy in your work?
- Are you married?
- Is your family large?

Students should conduct their interviews in English if possible. You may want them to work in pairs. Back in class, have students tell one or more classmates about the person they interviewed. Remind them to use contractions, for example:

> *I interviewed my neighbor. His name is Jerry. He's a dentist. His office is in Century City. His work is interesting and he's happy. Jerry isn't married. He's 27 years old. He's from Canada.*

If it isn't possible for your students to interview English-speakers, they can interview people in the language of their choice and report on the interview in English.

UNIT 6
The Present of *Be*: Questions with *Where*; Prepositions of Place

Unit Overview

In Unit 6 students will learn the use of questions with *Where is / Where are* and the use of prepositions to describe locations.

Grammar in Context (pages 39–40)

Comprehension Questions
- Why is Yuko having a party? (*It's her birthday.*)
- Where is Yuko's apartment? (*on First Avenue*)
- Which floor is she on? (*the second*)
- When is the party? (*Saturday*)

Words and Expressions
- Use the new words in questions about the students' lives, for example:
  —What is the name of your supermarket?
  —Do you go to a gym? Where is it?
  —Where is the library?
  —Do you live in an apartment building?
- Practice *See you* and *See you tomorrow* at the end of the class period.
- Give more examples of *by the way*. Help students understand that this expression is used to signal a digression or different topic. Illustrate this with a gesture: As you're talking about one topic, move your hand in a straight line in one direction. Then introduce a digression with *by the way*. Turn your hand in a different direction.

Working Together

Write the formula *at* + number + street on the board. Model your street address. Then go around the room and have each student say his or her address.

Grammar Presentation (pages 41–42)

Identify the Grammar

Where's her new apartment?
Her apartment is <u>on</u> First Avenue <u>between</u>
Jackson and Main.
It's <u>across from</u> a library and <u>next to</u> a gym.
She's <u>on</u> the second floor.

Grammar Charts

- Ask questions to help students notice the structures, for example:
  —*Where's* is short. What's the long form? *(where is)*
  —In plural questions, what word comes after *Where*? *(are)*
  —What kind of place comes after *on*? *(a street, a floor)*
  —What comes before and after *between*? *(names of streets)*
- Model questions with *Where is / Where are* _____ *from*? Then have students ask and answer the questions in pairs.
- Read the text beneath the map out loud. Have students repeat the sentences after you. Then have students cover the text and look only at the map. Ask questions, e.g.:
  —Where is the art museum?
  —What is it across from?
  —Where is the bank?
  —Where is the restaurant?

Grammar Notes

Notes 1 and 2   *(Exercises 2–4)*

- Write the prepositions from Note 2 on the board.
- Conduct short dialogues in which students use the prepositions to describe the location of your school or classroom. Point to the prepositions as students form their sentences. They should follow the model sentences in the text. Provide a model if none is given, for example:
  T: Where's our classroom?
  S1: It's in (city).
  S2: It's on (street).
  S3: It's at (address).

Note 3   *(Exercises 2–4)*

- Following the example sentences, tell students the location of your house or apartment. Call on a student to do the same.
- Put students in pairs to do the same.

Note 4   *(Exercises 2–4)*

- Practice by asking about rooms and facilities in your building, e.g.:
  —Where's the language lab? It's on the second floor.
  —Where's the office? It's on the first floor.
- If students are familiar with any numbered streets in your area, ask questions about places on those streets. Encourage students to answer without saying *street* or *avenue*, e.g.:
  T: Where's the coffee shop?
  Ss: On Third and Jefferson.
  T: Where's City Hall?
  Ss: On First and Washington.

Note 5   *(Exercise 4)*

Go around the room and have students say where they live and which bus people should take to get to their homes. Encourage them to use additional verbs they know, such as *get on, get off, go, walk, turn*, etc. For example:
  I live at 3550 Holloway Drive in West Hollywood. Take the number 3 bus. Get off at Fairfax Avenue. Walk two blocks north. Turn right. My building is next to the library. Come visit me!

Focused Practice (pages 42–44)

Exercise 3

corner: the place where two lines, walls, streets, etc., meet each other

Communication Practice (page 45)

Exercise 6

- Before listening, review the compass points with the students. Teach the words *north, south, east, west*. Have students point to those directions as you say them. You can also have students stand up and turn to face the direction you say.
- Students will also need to understand *northeast* for this activity. Choose an intersection from the map on page 43 and point out the northeast, northwest, southeast, and southwest corners. Then repeat the procedure above to reinforce.
- The recording also uses the word *down*. If students question the meaning, explain that *down* can mean movement in any direction away from the place where the speaker is standing. It can also mean that a person is

moving from a higher to a lower elevation, as in *going down a hill.*

Further Practice

Practice writing addresses. If your school is in North America, teach students how addresses are written in the United States and Canada. Explain about abbreviations and zip codes. Provide several models. Help students learn how to write their own addresses. Optionally, use several of the students' addresses for dictation. Check for proper form, capitalization, punctuation, and completeness. Follow up by having each student write a short letter to a secret partner in the class. Have students write their names and addresses on slips of paper and put the slips into a hat or box. Give each student an envelope. Have each student draw a name, write a short letter to the person whose name they drew, address the envelope correctly, and give you the letter.

GRAMMAR OUT OF THE BOX . . . . .

When all the letters are in, play the role of "mail carrier" and deliver each letter to its addressee.

Neighborhood map activity. Have students draw maps of their neighborhoods. They should write in the names of the streets and draw in the buildings. They should label some, but not all, of the buildings. At the bottom of their papers, underneath the maps, they should list the names of the unlabeled buildings, e.g., *my house, drug store, carpet store, bus stop,* etc. Put students in pairs. They should ask their partners to describe the locations of the buildings listed at the bottom of their maps. After they hear a location described, they should point to the correct building, and the speaker should confirm the listener's choice. For example:

S1: Where's the pet store?

S2: It's on Mason Street between Jackson and Howard, next to the bank, across from the Indian food store.

S1: Here? [pointing]

S2: Yes.

The Past of *Be*: Statements, *Yes / No* Questions

UNIT 7

Unit Overview

In Unit 7 students will learn the past of *be* in affirmative and negative statements and in *yes / no* questions.

Grammar in Context (pages 49–50)

Comprehension Questions

• Who was at Kathy's house last night? *(Josh and Amanda)*
• Where was Kathy last night? *(at the movies)*
• How was the movie? *(great, exciting, funny)*

Words and Expressions

• Extend the words list by eliciting other adjectives for describing movies. Ask the class if they have seen a certain movie. Then ask how it was. List the adjectives on the board, e.g., *boring, interesting, slow, stupid, violent, confusing, noisy, long.*
• Elicit other answers that match the question *How's it going?* For example: *OK, so-so, not so good, awful.* Demonstrate follow-up questions, e.g.:

T: How's it going?

S: Not so good.

T: Why? What's wrong?

S: I have a cold.

• Ask students where they were last night. Demonstrate answers similar in pattern to *at the movies,* e.g., *at home, at a friend's house, at the library,* etc.

Working Together

Part A
Have two students perform the dialogue as a role play in front of the class. Then have students do it in pairs.

Part B
After students practice, have several pairs perform their conversations for the class. To make the activity more challenging, have them do it without reading.

- What is Barcelona? (*a city in Spain*)
- Who was Mark's guide? (*Kathy, Amanda's friend*)

Words and Expressions

- Ask students to use the new words to describe today's weather in the place where you are. Then ask them to guess the weather in their home towns.
- Teach students how to say "It's 77 degrees (Fahrenheit). It's 25 degrees (Celsius)."
- Ask a student to leave the classroom. When he or she returns, say "Welcome back."
- Ask students if they remember some old fads or fashions. Examples: "Remember disco music? Remember the Macarena, Tamogochi™, Pokémon™?"

Working Together

Follow up Part B by asking if any student has been in the Prado. Also ask them to share what they know about these artists. You can also ask questions about the painting, e.g., "Who are these people? Where are they? Are they rich?" etc.

Grammar Presentation (page 58)

Identify the Grammar

How was your vacation?
Where were you?
How long were you there?
Who was your guide?

Grammar Charts

- Write the examples of the target grammar from the reading on the board.
- Ask questions to help students recognize the word order of the questions (*Wh- word + verb + subject*)
- Elicit long and short answers to the questions on the board. Encourage students to invent their own answers.
- Explain the meaning of "*Wh-* questions about the subject," i.e., the answer to the question is the subject of the answer sentence. You can display this by writing the question and short answer from the second chart on the board, then circling the word *Who* and drawing an arrow to the answer, *Mark*.

Grammar Notes

Note 1 (*Exercises 2–4*)
Do a chain drill in which students ask each other about their weekends and give short answers. Encourage them to give a variety of short answers, e.g.:

T: How was your weekend?

S1: Great. How was your weekend?

S2: Interesting. How was your weekend? . . .

Notes 2–6 (*Exercises 2–4*)
- Ask one student questions about his or her vacation. Use the questions in the text, i.e., *Where were you? When were you there? Who were you with? How was your vacation? How long was it? How was the weather?*
- Have the class ask you the same questions about a recent vacation of yours.
- Have students repeat the conversation in pairs.
- A twist on this activity is to provide answers and have students respond with the questions. For example:

T: my mother

Ss: Who was with you?

Focused Practice (pages 59–60)

Exercise 2
musician: someone who plays a musical instrument very well or as a job.

Communication Practice (pages 60–61)

Exercise 5
After listening, have students work in pairs to reconstruct the conversation between Mark and Jason, using the answers to the three questions.

Exercise 6
Say and have students repeat the days of the week. Recite them enough so that students memorize them. Then ask a few questions, such as "What day is today? What day is your favorite TV show? What day is your birthday this year?" etc.

Further Practice

Students should bring photos, postcards, and memorabilia from an outing or a vacation. Note: If you think this will be too similar to the activity in Unit 4, page 24, an alternative is to have students bring in magazine photos of fantasy vacation spots. Students can pretend to be rich jet-setters and make up imaginary answers to their partners' questions. On the board write the words *Who, What, When, Where, How, How long*. These words will serve as prompts for discussion. Have students sit in groups and talk about their vacations and their photos. Encourage them to use both present and past forms of *be*.

Weather report. Large newspapers generally provide information about the weather in major cities around the world. Find such a newspaper and create an information gap activity. Students can work as a whole class or in smaller groups. Give one card to each student. Write or photocopy the weather information about cities on separate cards. Make enough cards for all the students in a group or the class. Include both today's and yesterday's weather. Students should take turns describing the weather in their cities. For example: *My city is Cairo. Today it is 86 degrees. It is sunny and windy. Yesterday it was 84 degrees, and it was cloudy.* Listeners should take notes in a chart like the one below. For example:

City	Today's tempurature	Today's weather	Yesterday's temperature	Yesterday's weather
Cairo	86°F	sunny and windy	84°F	cloudy

UNIT 9 | The Simple Present: Statements

Unit Overview

In Unit 9 students will learn the use of the simple present in affirmative and negative statements.

Grammar in Context (pages 65–66)

Comprehension Questions

• Who needs more coffee? *(Judy)*
• Who has photos? *(Mark)*
• Who lives in Kenya? *(Mark's brother / Nick)*
• Who speaks Chinese? *(Mark)*
• Who speaks Swahili? *(Mark's brother / Nick)*

Words and Expressions

• Ask students questions using the new words, for example:
  —Do you have a brother or a sister? Do you look alike?
  —Do you go online every day?
  —Do you like to read novels?
  —Do you like to read newspapers in English?
  —What's your favorite magazine?
• Walk around the room and pretend to be a server at a restaurant. Follow the script in the Expressions box. After you have modeled the first conversation several times, call on students to play the role of servers.
• Ask students questions about their hobbies, vacations, jobs, etc. Respond with "That sounds interesting." Tell the class something unusual about yourself. Have them respond with the same phrase.

Working Together

Part B
Elicit other famous pairs of siblings and have students form similar sentences about them.

Grammar Presentation (pages 67–68)

Identify the Grammar

I _need_ more coffee.
He _lives_ in Kenya. He _teaches_ English there.
We both _have_ dark brown hair.
I _don't like_ computers.
Nick _doesn't like_ parties.

Grammar Charts

• Write the examples of the target grammar from the reading on the board.
• Read each sentence on the board and ask students to identify the subject and the verb.

Underline the verbs. Ask questions to help students recognize the irregular pattern. Have them look at the affirmative sentences and ask:
—Which verb is different from the base form? *(comes)*
—Which person is it? *(third-person singular)*
• Now have students look at the negative sentences. Ask, "Which verb form has an *-s* in it?" *(third-person singular)*
• At this point try to elicit the third-person *-s* rule from the students. Ask, "When do we use *-s* in the simple present?" *(third-person singular, affirmative and negative)*

Grammar Notes

Note 1 *(Exercises 2–4)*
• Give additional examples from your own life. Include both facts and things that happen habitually. Write the verbs on the board as you speak, for example:

Say	Write
I live alone.	*live*
I work eight hours every day.	*work*
I come from Texas.	*come*
Texas has a lot of oil.	*has*
I need a new car.	*need*
I call my father every day.	*call*

• Point to a verb on the board and point to a student. Have students make true sentences about themselves.

Note 2 *(Exercises 2–4)*
• Say a verb and a pronoun. Have students respond with the proper form of the verb. Drill all the pronouns quickly. Then switch verbs, for example:

T: work, I	Ss: I work.
T: work, you	Ss: You work.
T: work, he	Ss: He works.
T: read, I	Ss: I read.

• On the board draw a two-column chart like the one below. Elicit verbs from the students that take the *-es* and *-s* endings. Examples are provided below. Model the pronunciation of the words.

-es	*-s*
kiss	stop
teach	kick
wash	eat
fix	need
buzz	learn
go	sing

→ For additional practice, see the Supplementary Activities on page 89.

Note 3 *(Exercises 3–4)*
Do a series of drills to help students master the form and pronunciation of the negative.
• Provide a verb, say a pronoun, and have students respond with the uncontracted negative, e.g.:

T: speak, I	Ss: I do not speak.
T: speak, you	Ss: You do not speak.

• Say an uncontracted form. Students respond with the contracted form.

T: I do not speak Chinese.	Ss: I don't speak Chinese.
T: You do not understand.	Ss: You don't understand.

• Say an affirmative sentence. Students transform it to the negative with contractions.

T: I like chocolate.	Ss: I don't like chocolate.
T: Mimi and Raoul live in Spain	Ss: Mimi and Raoul don't live in Spain

Note 4 *(Exercise 4)*
• Demonstrate the use of *have* with all pronouns. A good context is modes of transportation, e.g.:
—I have a bicycle.
—My husband has a new car.
—We have an old van.
—My neighbors have a boat.
—You have a motorcycle, right?
• Ask students to raise their hands if they have a car, a bicycle, or a motorcycle. Tell students to look around to see who raises hands. Then elicit sentences from the students about their classmates *(Kim has a car, Susanna doesn't have a bicycle)*.

Focused Practice *(pages 68–71)*

Exercise 1
snow: when it snows, soft white pieces of frozen water fall from the sky

Exercise 3
a soda: a sweet drink that has bubbles in it

Exercise 5
usually: used when describing what happens most of the time; generally

Communication Practice (pages 71–73)

Exercise 6

Have students examine the map before listening. Help them understand where Romania is. If necessary, bring in a map of Europe. Ask other questions to see what students know about Romania, e.g., what language is spoken there, the main religion, neighboring countries, etc.

Exercise 7

for the moment: happening now but maybe not in the future

graphic artist: someone who draws pictures or designs as his or her job

advertising agency: a company that uses notices, photographs, etc., to try to persuade people to buy, do, or use something

Have students read the conversation before listening and try to predict which words fit in the blanks. Then have them listen to check their guesses.

Exercise 8

Part B

Put students in groups of three. Repeat the activity three times. Students should alternate taking the A, B, and C roles. To make the activity more authentic, Student C should not listen while Students A and B are talking.

Further Practice

In our materialistic world it is often difficult to distinguish between our wants and our needs. In this activity students will discuss this topic in small groups. Have students fill out a chart like the one below.

I really need	I really want
1.	1.
2.	2.
3.	3.

Have students share their answers with their classmates. Teach them to challenge each other, e.g.:

S1: I really need a car.

S2: You don't need a car. You can take the bus.

S1: I really want a new pair of boots.

S2: Why? Your old boots are good.

GRAMMAR OUT OF THE BOX ......

Card game. Have students play a modified version of the card game "Go Fish." The objective is for students to obtain all four cards of a kind (for example, four *2*s, four aces) by asking their classmates for them. Teach students the names of the ace and the face cards (jack, queen, king). Have students sit in groups of three or four. One student should be the dealer. The dealer shuffles the cards and gives each player eight cards. The remaining cards are placed in the center of the table. Students take turns asking each other for cards. They say, *Jacob, I need queens.* If Jacob has queens, he gives them to the requester, and the requester gets another turn. If Jacob has no queens, he says, *I don't have queens. Go fish.* The requester then takes a card from the center pile. When all the cards in the pile are used up, players continue asking each other for cards. When a player has all four cards of a kind, he or she lays them on the table. The first student to get rid of all his or her cards is the winner.

UNIT 10 The Simple Present: *Yes / No* Questions

Unit Overview

In Unit 10 students will learn how to form present *yes / no* questions and short answers.

Grammar in Context (pages 74–75)

Comprehension Questions

• Who needs a haircut? *(Mark)*
• Who is Marcello? *(a hairstylist)*
• Does he charge a lot? *(No, he's reasonable.)*

Words and Expressions

• Ask students real questions about their hair, e.g., who has their hair colored, who has highlights, who cuts their hair.
• You may need to explain the difference between a barber and a hairstylist. Generally a barber cuts men's hair and nothing else. A hairstylist serves both men and women and does color and styling in addition to cutting.

- At the beginning of class or when you meet students in the hallway, ask them, *What's up?* This provides a natural context for the phrase. You can also teach replies other than *Nothing much,* such as *Everything's fine, I got a new car,* etc.

Working Together

Part B

- Say and have the class repeat the items in the box.
- Expand the conversation by using language from the Expressions box. For example:

A: Do you know a good doctor?

B: I think so.

A: Does he charge a lot?

B: Yes, he does. He's expensive. But he's very good.

A: Do you have his phone number?

B: Sure. Hold on. I'll get it.

Grammar Presentation (page 76)

Identify the Grammar

Do you know a good barber?
Does he charge a lot?
Do you have his phone number?
Do you really think so?

Grammar Charts

- To demonstrate the use of *do* in questions, it is helpful to make the presentation visual. Take the examples of the target grammar from the reading and write each word of each sentence in big letters on a piece of construction paper. Use a different color for the word *do*. Fasten the pieces to the board in random order. (You can also do this on an overhead transparency.)
- By moving the pieces of paper around, form the statement *you know a good barber*. Ask the class: "Is this a statement or a question?" *(statement)* Now take the paper with the word *do* and place it in front of the other words. Again ask: "Is this a statement or a question?" *(question)*
- Repeat with the second sentence.
- Repeat this process but change the kernel sentences to "Does he know a good barber?" and "Does he have his phone number?"
- Elicit from students the rules regarding:
  —the placement of *do* in questions
  —the use of *does* in the third-person singular

Grammar Notes

Note 1 *(Exercises 2–5)*
- Drill the use of *do / does* in questions as follows:

T: I	Ss: Do I
T: you	Ss: Do you
T: he	Ss: Does he

- Expand by adding verbs and eliciting full questions, for example:

| T: I know Spanish. | Ss: Do I know Spanish? |
| T: He knows a good doctor. | Ss: Does he know a good doctor? |

Note 2 *(Exercises 2–3)*
Create a chart like the one below. Students work in pairs. Have them take turns forming questions using the cues in the chart. They can mix the verbs and nouns in any way they like. They should answer with short answers. For example:

A: Do you know a good hairstylist?

B: No, I don't. / Yes, I do.

know	doctor
have	hairstylist
need	appointment
want	phone number
like	dentist
	roommate

Focused Practice (pages 77–79)

Exercise 1
yoga: a system of exercises in which you control your body and your mind

Exercise 2
cost: to have a particular price

Exercise 3
work out: to do a set of exercises for your body regularly

mall: a very large building with a lot of stores inside it

Exercise 4
classical: classical music or art is serious and important

tank: a large container for holding liquid or gas

Communication Practice (pages 80–81)

Exercise 7
- *The game* refers to a team sport such as football, baseball, basketball, etc.
- Follow up on the listening by having students in pairs practice the conversation.

Exercise 8
- Expand Part A by having students write a few additional questions. A total of eight to ten provides more variety.
- A variation of Part B is to say the name of a student and have the class make sentences about that person, e.g.:

  T: Anna

  S1: She likes chocolate.

  S2: She doesn't like the rain.

  S3: She knows a good joke.

Further Practice
Play a version of "What's My Line?" The purpose of this game is to guess someone's profession. Make a handout or an overhead transparency with a list of the occupations that the students have learned. Following is a partial list; elicit others from the students and add them to the list.

actor	mechanic	student
cashier	movie star	teacher
doctor	nurse	tour guide
engineer	painter	travel agent
graphic artist	police officer	writer
hairstylist	singer	

Have one student think of a profession. Then have other students ask *yes / no* questions, for example:
- Do you wear a uniform?
- Do you work outdoors?
- Do you work alone?
- Do you work with food?
- Are you an artist?

The class has only three chances to guess what the student's occupation is. (This prevents students from asking repeatedly *Are you a carpenter? Are you a dog catcher?* etc. Encourage students to gather as much information as possible about the job before guessing what it is.) Then have the class select three students to ask questions. If they all guess incorrectly, they "lose." This game can also be played in small groups.

GRAMMAR OUT OF THE BOX ......

Making an appointment. Have students role-play making an appointment for a service they need—a haircut, manicure, car repair, tutoring, delivery, etc. In newspapers, local magazines, or the Yellow Pages of the phone book, find authentic advertisements for services. Put students in pairs. One student will play the role of the person seeking the service. The other student will be the service provider (or the person who answers the phone at the service provider's office). Instruct students to write a script for their phone conversation. They can use Exercise 5, page 79, as a model. Of course, they should substitute authentic information for the names and times in the model. Teach students strategies to use if they don't understand the person they are speaking with on the phone. These include asking the speaker to slow down, repeat, or spell words. Have pairs practice their conversations and then perform them in front of the class. If possible, have students make actual appointments for services they need. Have them report back to you with the following information:

Type of service: _____
Name of provider: _____
Phone number: _____
Location: _____
Day and time of appointment: _____

UNIT 11 — The Simple Present: *Wh-* Questions

Unit Overview

In Unit 11 students will learn how to ask and answer *wh-* questions in the simple present.

Grammar in Context (pages 82–83)

Comprehension Questions
- How does Yoshio like the United States? (*He likes it a lot.*)
- Where is Yoshio from? (*Japan*)
- What does Yoshio's father do? (*He's a businessman.*)
- When does the calculus class start? (*at 2:30*)

Words and Expressions

Do a class survey and tally the results on the board.

- Ask questions like the following:
  —Who goes to bed early?
  —Who stays up late?
  —Who gets up early?
  —Who sleeps in on weekends?
- Count the number of people in the class. Then write the results on the board like this:
  —*go to bed early: 5/20*
  —*stay up late: 15/20*
- Ask the students if they are surprised by the results.
- Have students practice making invitations and responding with *let's go*. This can be done in a chain as follows:

T: see a movie

S1: Do you want to see a movie together?

S2: Sure. Let's go.

T: go to the beach

S2: Do you want to go to the beach together?

S3: Sure. Let's go.

T: do homework together

etc.

Working Together

- Students can switch partners for each part of this activity.
- For Part B, encourage students to use the expression *me too*.

Grammar Presentation (page 84)

Identify the Grammar

How do you like the United States?
What time do people go to bed there?
Why does he stay up so late?
What does he do?
What else is different?

Grammar Charts

- Have students read all the sentences in the first chart. Ask the class:
  —When do we use *do*? *(with I, you, we, and they)*
  —When do we use *does*? *(with he, she, and it / with the third-person singular)*
- Next, ask students to identify the subject and base verb. *(They are the words after the wh-*

word and do. For example, in "How do I get there?" the subject is I and the base verb is get.)
- Now focus on the second chart. Help students recognize that *wh-* questions about the subject don't use *do / does*. Ask:
  —What are the verbs in these sentences? *(wakes and happens)*
  —Do we use *do* in these sentences? *(no)*

Grammar Notes

Note 1 *(Exercises 2–3)*
- Write a chart like the following on the board or on an overhead transparency:

who	by bus
what time	10:30 P.M.
when	because I get up early
why	6:30 A.M.
where	in Riverdale
how	with my husband and children

- Model the activity. Point to the first answer, *by bus*. Elicit the question, *How does the teacher get to school?*
- Have students take a minute to write a question to match each answer.
- Call on pairs of students to read the questions and answers. For example:

S1: Who does the teacher live with?

S2: She lives with her husband and children.

S3: What time does the teacher get up?

S4: She gets up at 6:30 A.M.

S5: When does the teacher go to bed?

S6: She goes to bed at 10:30 P.M.

Note 2 (Exercise 3)
- Students are likely to be confused about subject-pattern questions, and at first they will insert *do* into all *wh-* questions. Keep explaining that "a question about the subject" means a question about the subject of the *answer sentence*. For example:

Q: Who wakes you in the morning?

A: *My mother* wakes me up.

Q: What has eight legs?

A: *A spider* has eight legs.

- To elicit questions with *who has*, form a sentence about a distinguishing feature of

each student in the class. Students respond with the question. For example:
—Regina has green eyes. *(Who has green eyes?)*
—Janusch has a red backpack. *(Who has a red backpack?)*

• To elicit questions with *what* + verb, form sentences about animals and elicit the questions from the students. For example:
—A penguin has wings but cannot fly. *(What has wings but cannot fly?)*
—A bat has wings and flies but isn't a bird. *(What has wings and flies but isn't a bird?)*
—A whale lives in the ocean but it isn't a fish. *(What lives in the ocean but isn't a fish?)*
—A snake loves the sun but never gets sunburned. *(What loves . . . , etc.)*

Note 3 *(Exercise 3)*

• On the board or on a transparency, write the definitions of several high-frequency words the students are unlikely to know.
• Model *What does _____ mean?* and have students guess the proper definition. Do this for two or three words.
• For the remaining words, point to a student to ask the question. The class answers.

Focused Practice (pages 85–86)

Exercise 1

alarm clock: a clock that makes a loud noise at the time you want to wake up

boss: a person who is in charge and tells other people what work to do

Communication Practice (pages 87–88)

Exercise 5

After doing the activity according to the directions given, put students in pairs. Have them take turns reading the answers and eliciting the questions from one another.

Exercise 6

• To model, interview one of the students. Have the class repeat the questions after you to practice the proper intonation of the questions.
• As students work in pairs, circulate and help them with intonation.

Exercise 7

You can follow up on this activity in a number of ways:
• Have students write sentences using the words.
• Put students in pairs or small groups. Give them four or five of the words from the lists and instruct them to tell a short story using all the words.
• A few days after this activity, have students quiz each other on their recall of the words and definitions. They should follow the example on page 88 but select words at random from the two lists.

Further Practice

Have students write paragraphs following the model in Working Together, Part C, page 83. Tell students to mention their work schedules, what kind of people they deal with, any special equipment or uniforms they need, special training their jobs require, etc. Students can work alone or in pairs. Collect the paragraphs and correct them. Then, have students read their paragraphs to the class, and have the class guess what the job is.

GRAMMAR OUT OF THE BOX . . . . . .

General knowledge quiz.[1] Prepare a series of general-information questions and answers. Each question and each answer should be on a separate card or slip of paper. Sample questions:
• Who lives in the Vatican?
• What language do they speak in Brazil?
• When do kangaroos sleep?
Give each student a card or slip. Have students mingle. Those with questions search for the matching answer, and vice versa. As soon as students find each other, they sit down. Afterward pairs of students present their questions and answers to the whole class. This activity can be repeated with students writing their own *wh-* questions.

[1] Adapted from Penny Ur. *Grammar Practice Activities.* Cambridge, UK: Cambridge University Press, 1988.

UNIT 12 The Simple Present: *Be* and *Have*

Unit Overview

In Unit 12 students will learn how to use the verbs *be* and *have* in simple present statements and questions.

Grammar in Context (pages 89–90)

Comprehension Questions

- What does Sonia Jones look like? *(She has dark hair and dark eyes, she's tall and thin, and she's pregnant.)*
- How old is she? *(early 20s)*

Words and Expressions

- Use the words to describe several students in the class. Ask: "Who's tall? Who has brown hair?" etc.
- Ask a few students to describe their best friends. Ask: "What is his or her name? What does he or she look like? How old is he or she?"
- Find examples of students in the class who are 20-something, 30-something, etc.

Working Together

Part A
After students practice in pairs, call up one or two pairs to "perform" the conversation in front of the class.

Part B
Point out and explain the picture of the harpsichord. Define "child prodigy."

Part C
- Model answers to the questions by speaking about yourself.
- Students can do this activity in small groups.

Grammar Presentation (pages 91–92)

Identify the Grammar

She's in your class.
She has dark hair and dark eyes.
Almost everyone . . . is 20-something.
She has two heads.
Her phone number is . . .

Grammar Charts

- After reading the examples, review the forms of *be* and *have*. Say the pronouns (*I, you, he,* etc.) and have students provide the correct verb form.
- Elicit the context in which each verb is used. Ask questions such as the following:
—Which verb do we use with adjectives? *(be)*
—Which verb do we use with an adjective followed by a noun? *(have)*
—Which verb do we use with height? *(be)*
—Which verb do we use to talk about a person's eyes or hair? *(have)*
- Have students provide examples of the contexts above.

Grammar Notes

Note 1   *(Exercises 2–4)*
- Call up one student to stand before the class. Have the students form sentences following your cues. For example:

T: hair

Ss: Yoshi has black hair.

T: height

Ss: Yoshi is tall.

- An alternative activity, which involves more movement, is the following:
—On the board, write the words *hair, eyes, height*.
—Instruct students to mingle and find partners who are similar in one of the ways written on the board.
—When students have formed pairs or small groups, ask them to state how they are similar. For example: *We have brown hair. We are tall.*

Note 2   *(Exercise 2)*
- Do a transformation drill. Say the long form. Have students respond with the contraction. For example:

T: He is not home.

Ss: He isn't home.

T: I do not have a watch.

Ss: I don't have a watch.

- Put students in pairs. Instruct students to make three affirmative sentences about their partners using *be* and *have*. One sentence must be false. Go around the room and have students say their sentences. The class must correct the false statement. For example:

S1: Jacques is tall. He has blond hair. He has a car.

Ss: He doesn't have a car.

Note 3   *(Exercises 2–4)*
- Play a version of the game "20 Questions." Students must guess the identity of a mystery person by asking *yes / no* questions. The mystery person can be a student, a faculty member, or someone famous. Model by having a student pick a mystery person and asking questions yourself. For example:
  —Is the person a man?
  —Does he have brown hair?
  —Is he young?
  —Does he have glasses?
- Have students play in small groups. Circulate and provide help as needed.

Note 4   *(Exercises 2, 4)*
- Bring in magazine photos featuring people in various settings. To model the activity, hold up a picture and ask the students *wh-*questions. Encourage students to make up imaginative answers. Sample questions:
  —Where are the people?
  —Who is the old man?
  —What season is it?
  —What does the woman think of the man's hat?
  —Why does the child look sad?
- Put students in groups. Give each group a picture. Have them ask and answer questions about it. The questions should form a loose story.
- To conclude, have one person from each group show the picture to the class and tell the story that the group made up.

Note 5   *(Exercises 2, 4)*
Go around the room and have each student say his or her age. Example: *I am 22 years old.*

Focused Practice (pages 92–94)

Exercise 2

prodigy: a young person who is extremely good at doing something

talented: able to do something well

degree: an official piece of paper that says someone has completed his or her studies at a college, university, etc.

Communication Practice (pages 94–95)

Exercise 4
Ask students to describe the men before listening. To focus the activity, instruct them to look for differences in hair, size, and age. Teach the sentence, *He has a mustache.*

Exercise 5
Model by describing one of the men and having the class say which one it is.

Exercise 6
You may wish to do a vocabulary review prior to this activity. Put students in groups. Assign each group one of the categories: occupation, height, eye color, etc. The students' task is to list as many words as they can in their category. Give them about five minutes to create their lists. Then have a student from each group share the group's list with the class.

Further Practice
For homework, have students write a "Who Am I?" paragraph like the one on page 90. Collect the paragraphs and correct them. After students rewrite, post the paragraphs on the walls of the classroom. Students should circulate, read the paragraphs, and write the name of the person they think it is below the paragraph.

If students need help finding information about a person, have them do an Internet search for "Person's name" + biography. For example: "Elton John" + biography.[1]

Spot the differences game. In this game, students look at two pictures that differ in a limited number of details. They must find the differences and explain them to a partner. To find pictures, go on the Internet and search for "spot the differences" or "find the differences." Other sources are children's game books and magazines.[2] Put students in pairs. Have them work together to find the differences between their pictures. Most of the time the differences

---

[1] An excellent general-information site in easy English is http://simple.wikipedia.org

[2] *Life* magazine, included as a weekly insert in many newspapers in the United States, has such a puzzle on its last page nearly every week.

can be described using *be* or *have*. For example, "In picture 1 the boy has a balloon, but in picture 2 he has a ball." To make the activity more challenging, give one picture to Student A and another picture to Student B. They must ask each other questions to find the differences. For example, "Does the girl in your picture have blond hair?" Follow up by having students write sentences about the differences they found.

UNIT 13 Adverbs of Frequency

Unit Overview

In Unit 13 students will learn the meaning and position of adverbs of frequency in simple present sentences.

Grammar in Context (pages 96–97)

Comprehension Questions

• Why is Steve tired? *(He doesn't get enough sleep. He skips breakfast. He eats junk food. He doesn't exercise.)*
• When does Steve usually go to bed? *(at 12:30 or 1:00 A.M.)*
• Does Steve ever sleep late? *(Yes, sometimes on the weekend.)*

Words and Expressions

• Have students look at the pictures. Tell about yourself or ask questions to convey the meaning of the new words. For example:
 —What are some examples of *fast food?*
 —I eat breakfast every day. I never *skip* breakfast. How about you?
 —A big ice cream cone costs $2.00. I have $1.50. Is it *enough*?
• Make sentences in which you paraphrase *kind of*. For example: "I'm kind of tired today. I'm not very tired. I'm a little tired." Then ask students: "Are you very tired? Are you a little tired? Are you kind of tired?" Do the same with *hungry, sad,* or other adjectives.
• Give students a number of scenarios in which they might be *in a hurry*. Ask them what they do in those situations. For example:
 —You wake up late. You're in a hurry. Do you skip breakfast?
 —You're late to a movie. You're in a hurry. Do you take a taxi?

—You come home late from work. You don't have time to make dinner. You're in a hurry. Do you order a pizza?

Working Together

Part B
• Model sentences about the pictures with *never, sometimes,* and *often.* Tell students to pay attention to the position of these words in the sentence. For example: "I often eat vegetables. I never eat fish."
• Expand if necessary by teaching the words *(almost) always, usually, rarely.* Students may need these words to form truthful statements.

Grammar Presentation (pages 98–99)

Identify the Grammar

I <u>usually</u> stay up till 12:30 or 1:00.
Do you <u>ever</u> sleep late?
You <u>always</u> have fast food for lunch.
<u>Sometimes</u> it's junk food.
I <u>sometimes</u> skip breakfast.
I'm <u>always</u> in a hurry.

Grammar Charts

Ask questions to get students to notice the position of the adverbs. For example:
• How do we use *ever? (in questions)*
• Do frequency adverbs come before or after *be*? *(after)*
• Do frequency adverbs come before or after other verbs? *(before)*
• In short answers, where are the frequency adverbs? *(before do)*

Grammar Notes

Note 1 *(Exercises 2–3)*
• To help students learn the sequence of adverbs, from most often to least often, write each adverb on a piece of paper. Tape the pieces of paper randomly on the board. Call up a student to arrange the papers in the correct order.
• A variation is to put students in groups of six. Each student gets a paper with an adverb written on it. Instruct students to line up according to the frequency of the adverbs.

Note 2 *(Exercise 2)*
• You should still have the list of adverbs from Note 1 on the board. Write a set of adjectives next to the adverbs, like this:

Adverbs	Adjectives
always usually often sometimes etc.	late early tired happy etc.

- Have students "mix and match," making true sentences about themselves or people they know. For example: *I am never late to school. My father is always tired in the evening.*

Note 3 *(Exercises 2–3)*
- Repeat the procedure from Note 2 using other verbs the students know, e.g., *walk, work, eat,* etc. Once again elicit true sentences, e.g., *I always drive to school. I never walk. Jonas usually works on Friday after school.*
- To practice the various positions of *usually* and *sometimes*, put students in groups of four. Write the following sentences on the board. Give each student one of the sentences (substitute students' names).
  —Bella eats lunch at her desk.
  —Tanya exercises early in the morning.
  —Tomas reads in bed.
  —Antonio writes letters to his friends.
- Instruct students to take turns reading their sentences out loud. The person to their right should repeat the sentence, inserting *usually.* The next student should repeat the sentence but say *usually* in a different place. The third student should again repeat and put *usually* in a different position.
- Repeat the procedure with *sometimes.*

Notes 4 and 5 *(Exercise 2)*
- Write a set of interesting verb phrases on the board, e.g., *eat popcorn, fly first-class, go to the art museum, buy jewelry, babysit, forget the time, buy a gift for a friend, lie about your age.*
- Have students stand up. Give a tennis ball to a student. The student makes a question with *Do you ever . . . ?* and throws the ball to a classmate, who answers the question. That student then forms a new question and throws the ball to a different student. The game continues until everyone has asked and answered a question.

→ For additional practice, see the Supplementary Activities on page 90.

Focused Practice (pages 99–100)

Exercise 3
take a shower: wash yourself while standing under running water

on time: at the right time; not early, not late

Communication Practice (page 101)

Exercise 5
Have students read the incomplete sentences before listening. Elicit phrases that could possibly fit in the blanks. Students then listen to find out if they guessed correctly.

Exercise 6
If your class is large, Part B can be done in groups.

Further Practice
Have students re-read Exercise 1, page 99. Explain that they are going to write a similar paragraph about a classmate. The opening sentence should be the same: *(Classmate's name) has an active life.* Have students write six or seven questions based on the information in the paragraph as well as the questions in Exercise 2, page 99. For example: *When do you usually get up? Do you exercise before school? Do you ever feel tired? What do you usually eat for breakfast?* etc. Put students in pairs and have them interview each other. They should write their paragraphs for homework. After you have corrected the paragraphs, display them on the walls or bulletin board in your classroom.

GRAMMAR OUT OF THE BOX . . . . . .

A good teacher.[1] Create a questionnaire like the one on the next page. If you prefer, you can have students talk about "a good parent" and change the questions accordingly.[2]

[1] This activity is adapted from Penny Ur, *Grammar Practice Activities.* Cambridge, UK: Cambridge University Press, 1988.

[2] Other variations: Have students talk about hobbies, free-time activities such as watching television, or chores such as washing the car.

A good teacher How often does he or she ...	always	very often	often	sometimes	rarely	never
give homework?						
play games?						
make jokes?						
give punishments?						
give praise?						
criticize?						
get angry?						
smile?						
arrive late?						
Now answer the questions again for a bad teacher!						

Give each student a copy of the questionnaire. Go through the items and clarify vocabulary as needed. Then instruct students to answer the questions individually. Put them in small groups and have them compare answers. Remind them to interact by asking questions with *How often*.

UNIT 14 The Present Progressive: Statements

Unit Overview

In Unit 14 students will learn the meaning and use of the present progressive in affirmative and negative statements.

Grammar in Context (pages 105–106)

Comprehension Questions

- Where are Danny and Matt? *(at the video store)*
- What are they doing? *(They're looking at the new games.)*
- What is Jeremy doing? *(He's watching his brother and sister.)*
- Who is baking a cake? *(Jeremy's grandfather)*

Words

- Pantomime *look at* and *wait for*. For example, pretend you're in an art museum. Walk around and say, "I'm at an art museum. I'm looking at the paintings." Similarly, you could

pretend to be looking at a sporting event on television.
- Pantomime waiting for a bus. Look at your watch and say, for example, "I'm waiting for the bus. It's late."
- Model the pronunciation of *lasagna* and *vegetable soup*.

Expressions

- Elicit other expressions similar to *What's going on*, e.g., "What's happening? / What are you doing?"
- Have pairs of students role-play short dialogues with *What's going on?* To prepare, write actions on index cards, e.g., *watching television, cleaning the house, babysitting, doing homework*. Hand a card to one student in each pair. Tell the students to pretend they're talking on the phone. The student without a card asks, "What's going on?" The student with a card answers using the information on his or her card.
- On the board, write the following:

  A: ———

  B: ———

  A: ———

  B: ———

  A: Why don't you come on over?

  B: OK. Thanks. See you soon.

- Have students work in pairs to compose the missing lines. Then have them read their dialogues to the class.

Working Together

Part B
- Students should use their own names when role-playing the conversation.
- Instead of practicing with just one partner, the class can practice together by forming two concentric circles. The students on the inside circle should face the students on the outside. At a signal from you, the students on the inside should begin walking. The students on the outside should stand still. At another signal from you, the inside students should stand still, face the person opposite them, and begin the conversation. At another signal from you, the whole sequence should be repeated.

Grammar Presentation (pages 107–108)

Identify the Grammar

- *Hiro's studying*.
- *Ron isn't studying*.
- *We're looking* at the new games.
- *I'm watching* my sister and brother.

Grammar Charts

- Have students read the charts both vertically and horizontally. Then ask questions targeting the form of the present progressive, for example:
  —In all forms of the present progressive, what is the ending on the verb? *(-ing)*
  —Which form of *be* is used with *I / he / it / we / they*? *(am, is, is, are, are)*
  —Which word do we use in a negative present progressive verb? *(not)*
  —What is the position of *not*? *(after be and before verb + -ing)*
  —How many contractions of *I am not* are there? *(one)*
  —How many contractions of *He is not* are there? *(two)*
  —How many contractions of *We are not* are there? *(two)*
- Reinforce the meaning of the present progressive. Write the examples of the target grammar from the reading on the board. Refer to the sentences and ask, for example: "When is Hiro studying?" Elicit the answer *(now)*. Do this for all the sentences on the board.

Grammar Notes

Notes 1–3   *(Exercises 2–5)*

- Walk around the room and perform a variety of actions. Narrate using the present progressive. Use contractions, e.g.: "I'm opening the window. / I'm erasing the board. / I'm turning on the light."
- Choose a student to do actions with you. Narrate with *we* as you act: "We're walking. / We're erasing the board. / We're sitting down."
- Now choose a student to perform actions. The class should narrate as the student does things, for example: "He's opening the window. / He's cleaning his glasses. / He's sitting on the desk."

Note 2   *(Exercises 2–5)*

- Write the following chart on the board or on an overhead transparency.

1	2
listen	read
talk	answer
write	underline
run	jog
grow	snow
fix	tax
play	pay

- Use the words in column 1 as a model. Write the *-ing* forms next to the base forms. Elicit the rules from the students.
- Have students write the *-ing* forms of the words in column 2. Then call individuals up to the board to write the words. Correct as needed.
- Elicit other words that follow each of the rules illustrated in the chart. Add the words to the chart.

Note 4   *(Exercises 2–5)*

- Pantomime a number of affirmative-negative pairs. Narrate your actions. For example:
  —I'm eating. I'm not drinking.
  —I'm reading. I'm not writing.
- Do the same to illustrate verbs with *is* and *are*. (See Notes 1–3.) Have a student perform actions with you and say, for example, *We're sitting. We're not standing*. Have a student perform several actions and elicit sentences such as *He's listening. He's not talking*.
- Do a transformation / substitution drill in order to practice the two forms of the negative with *is* and *are*. Say an affirmative sentence. Then point to students to give the two negative forms. For example:

  —T: Bjorn is studying.

  S1: He isn't studying.

  S2: He's not studying.

  —T: Maryam and Ilsa are eating lunch.

  S3: They aren't eating lunch.

  S4: They're not eating lunch.

Note 5

- Write the following sentences on the board. Draw a large circle around them, and draw a diagonal line through the circle so that it resembles a "No Smoking" or "No Parking" sign. It should be absolutely clear to students that these sentences are wrong.

—*Jonas is being a teacher.*
—*Fatima is liking bananas.*
—*Steven isn't having a cell phone.*
—*I am needing a dictionary.*
—*Patil isn't wanting dessert.*

- Call on students to correct each sentence orally. Then have them come up to the board, write the correct sentence next to the wrong one, and erase the wrong one.
- Underline the verbs *be, like, have, need,* and *want.* Elicit two or three sentences using each verb.

Note 6 *(Exercise 3)*
- Pantomime two actions. Students form a sentence with *and.* For example: "You're brushing your hair and putting on lipstick."
- Call on student volunteers to pantomime. The class responds with sentences.

Focused Practice (pages 109–112)

Exercise 1
baggy: baggy clothes fit very loosely

allergy: a condition that makes you ill when you eat, touch, or breathe in a particular thing

Exercise 4
suit: a set of clothes made from the same material, including a short coat and pants or a skirt

casual: casual clothes are clothes that you wear at home, not at work or at school

turtleneck sweater: a sweater with a high, close-fitting collar that covers most of your neck

policy: a plan that is agreed to by a political party, government, or company

Communication Practice (pages 113–114)

Exercise 7
- Before listening, have students look at the pictures of the rooms and name each one. Also elicit some of the activities that people do in each room.
- After listening, ask students to explain the difference between *cooking* and *baking.* Also explain *gardening.*

Exercise 8
As a variation, turn this into a listening activity as follows:
- Put students in pairs.
- Student 1 says all the sentences that are true for him or her.

- Student 2 checks what he or she heard. Then the students switch.
- Have partners switch books and make sure each one checked the correct items.

Exercise 9
Extend this activity by having students take turns describing a "mystery" person in the class.

Exercise 10
Encourage students to take photos of locations outside the class, such as their apartments, a garden, etc. They can talk about what people are doing / not doing as well as the weather, e.g.: "The sun is shining. / It's not raining."

Further Practice
Bring in pictures showing many things going on—street scenes, a busy office, a sporting event, etc. The pictures should be large enough so that the whole class can see them, or you can divide students into small groups and give a different picture to each group. Distribute the pictures facedown. At your signal, students turn over the picture and examine it for one minute. Then take away the picture or have students turn it over again. Immediately have students write everything they can remember about the picture, using the present progressive. You can turn this into a competition by giving a time limit. When time is up, have students read their sentences. The person or team who remembered the most details is the winner.

GRAMMAR OUT OF THE BOX ......

Concentration. To play this memory game, you will need sets of cards made up of matched pairs of identical pictures. Each pair of pictures shows a person or an animal doing a recognizable activity. You will need at least 20 pairs, which you can make by drawing stick figures or by downloading pictures from clip-art sites on the Internet. To play the game, students work in small groups (three or four students). Each group has a set of cards. These are randomly distributed on a table or the floor, facedown. The first participant turns over two cards and says what is happening in each. For example: "He is running. / She is brushing her teeth." If the cards do not match, the student turns them back facedown, and the next student has a turn. The aim is for students to remember where the matching cards are located. If a student turns over matching cards, he or she keeps them. At the end of the game, the student with the most pairs is the winner.

UNIT 15 The Present Progressive: Yes / No Questions

Unit Overview

In Unit 15 students will learn present progressive *yes / no* questions and short answers.

Grammar in Context (pages 115–116)

Comprehension Questions

- What special day is it for Tim and Jessica? *(their anniversary)*
- Where are they? *(at a restaurant)*
- Who's babysitting? *(Kelly Brown)*
- What is Ben doing? *(baking cookies)*
- What are Annie and Gail doing? *(probably studying)*

Words

- Hold up your book, point to each picture, say each word, and have the class repeat.
- Ask questions using the new words. (Note: It is fine to ask questions using the simple present. If students make errors, do not correct them at this time.) For example:
  —What's your favorite meal?
  —What time do you eat breakfast / lunch / dinner?
  —Do you like to eat breakfast?
  —When is your (your parents') anniversary?
  —How often do you get a haircut?

Expressions

- Have students practice reading the short dialogues in pairs.
- Give students copies of the dialogues, but replace the sentences without the expressions with a blank, for example:

  A: _____?
  B: Yes, but I'll check on them.

- Put students in pairs and have them write their own missing lines of dialogue. Then call on pairs of students to read their dialogues out loud.

Working Together

- Explain "Dennis the Menace." It is a classic American cartoon about a five-year-old boy, Dennis. He is very cute but also quite annoying. (Note: A *menace* is someone or something that causes damage or is annoying.)
- Make sure students understand that *babysitter* and *sitter* are the same thing.
- Ask students questions to help the class understand the cartoon. For example:
  —Who are the man and woman? *(Dennis's parents)*
  —What time is it, probably? *(late)*
  —Who is sleeping on the couch? *(the babysitter)*
  —Why does Dennis want money? *(Because he is "babysitting" the babysitter.)*

Grammar Presentation (page 117)

Identify the Grammar

- *Is Jeremy watching Ben and Annie?*
- *Are the children listening to you?*
- *Are you helping Ben with his math?*
- *Is Annie studying for her science test?*

Grammar Charts

- Ask students to tell you the word order of *yes / no* questions in the present progressive. Elicit *am / is / are* + subject + verb *-ing*.
- Write the examples from the reading on the board. Ask students to answer the questions according to the reading. *(No, he isn't* OR *No, he's not*, etc.)
- Review the fact that there are two negative forms with *is* and *are*.
- Help students notice that the short answers in the present progressive are the same as the short answers to present questions with *be*. Ask students contrasting questions with the same answers, for example:
  —Is it cold?
    Yes, it is. / No, it isn't / No, it's not.
  —Is it raining?
    Yes, it is. / No, it isn't. / No, its not.

Grammar Notes

Note 1 *(Exercises 2–4)*
Do a transformation drill. Say statements. Have students change them to questions. For example:

T: She's wearing a hat.

Ss: Is she wearing a hat?

Notes 2–3 *(Exercises 2–3)*
- List various hours of the day on the board, e.g.:

A.M.	P.M.
6, 8:30, 11:00	1:00, 3:15, 5:00, 6:00, 9:00

- Tell the class what day of the week it is. Point to different times and have students ask you questions about what you are doing. They need to keep asking until they get the right answer. For example:

T: It's Wednesday. [Point to 3:15 P.M.]

S1: Are you planning lessons for the next day?

T: No, I'm not.

S2: Are you driving home?

T: No, I'm not.

S3: Are you jogging?

T: Yes, I am.

- Select one student to come up before the class and mimic what you have done, first writing times on the board, then answering the class's questions about what he or she is doing. Monitor students' answers for correct use of contractions.

→ For additional practice, see the Supplementary Activities on page 91.

Focused Practice (pages 117–119)

Exercise 3

a romance: a story about love between two people

awesome: very impressive; extremely good

kidding: saying something to someone as a joke

exist: be real or alive

Exercise 4

celebrate: have a special meal or party because of a particular event

Communication Practice (pages 120–121)

Exercise 6

Have students read the questions before listening. If necessary, review who Tim is.

Exercise 7

- Put students in pairs. To make this activity more interactive, have only one student in each pair look at the cartoon and write questions.
- Next, the other student looks at the cartoon for 10 seconds.
- Finally, Student 1 reads the questions and Student 2 answers with short answers, using contractions when possible.

Exercise 8

Tell students to write their sentences in the first person, e.g., "I am cooking an omelet."

Further Practice

Repeat the activity for Notes 2–3 with some variations. Put students in small groups. Instruct each student to make a two-column table like the one used for the Notes and to fill in several A.M. and P.M. times. Students take turns answering their classmates' questions. The student who is answering should point to a time, say what day it is, and state where he or she is. For example:

S1: It's 9 P.M., December 25. I am at home in Barcelona.

S2: Are you having dinner with your family?

S1: Yes, I am.

GRAMMAR OUT OF THE BOX . . . . . .

Guessing mimes. Make a list of actions to be mimed. Cut them into strips and put the strips in a hat or box. See the list below. In class, a student pulls a strip out and mimes the action written there. The other students ask questions about what the student is doing. For example:
- Are you eating something?
- Are you opening something?
- Are you riding a bicycle?

Make sure students continue to ask questions throughout the mime. Don't allow a long period of silence to pass.

UNIT 16 The Present Progressive: *Wh-* Questions

Unit Overview

In Unit 16 students will learn about *wh-* questions in the present progressive.

Grammar in Context (pages 122–123)

Comprehension Questions

• Where is Annie's father going? *(to the store)*
• Why is he going there? *(to buy milk)*
• What is Jessica making? *(tacos and beans)*
• Who's staying for dinner? *(Yoshio)*

Words

• Say and have students repeat the foods shown in the pictures. Help with pronunciation.
• Then ask questions about each of the foods. For example:
  —What country is (spaghetti) from?
  —What is in it (What are the ingredients)?
  —How do you cook it?
  —Do you like it?

Expressions

• Have pairs of students read each short dialogue. Ask students to explain or paraphrase the boldfaced expressions. For example, "We're out of milk" could be "We don't have milk." "Come on!" is said when we don't believe someone. "Why don't you . . ." is a suggestion.
• After listening, put students in pairs again. Have them write their own short dialogues with the new expressions. They should use the dialogues in the book as models. For example:

A: Why is Mika going to the store?
B: We're out of shampoo.

• Have pairs of students read their dialogues to the class.

Working Together

• Have students work in pairs. Model the activity with a student as follows: Point to a picture. The student says what the person is eating. Then the student points to a picture and you say what the person is eating.
• Have students continue in pairs.

Grammar Presentation (page 124)

Identify the Grammar

• *Where's he going?*
• *Why is he going to the store now?*
• *Who are you talking to?*
• *What are you making?*
• *What's he doing?*

Grammar Charts

• Write the examples from the reading on the board. Call on students to ask the questions and to give answers according to the reading. Ask students to expand each answer to a full sentence. Write the full sentence on the board and underline the part of the sentence that answers each question, as follows:
  —*He's going to the store.*
  —*He's going to the store now because we're out of milk.*
  —*I'm talking to Dad.*
  —*I'm making tacos and beans.*
  —*He's writing a report.*
• Ask students if the underlined phrases are before or after the verb. *(after; They are part of the verb phrase or the complement.)* This will help students understand the meaning of "*Wh-* Questions about the Object."
• Have students focus on the word order of the *wh-* questions. Ask:
  —Is the word order of *wh-* questions and *yes / no* questions the same or different? *(same)*
  —Where is the *wh-* word? *(at the beginning)*
  —Where is the subject? *(after am / is / are)*

Grammar Notes

Notes 1–4   *(Exercises 2–3)*

- On the board, write: *what, where, why, who, how*
- Ask the class: Who has a grandmother / father?
- Choose one student and ask him or her for the name of his or her grandparent. Then point to the *wh-* words on the board and ask present progressive questions about the grandparent. Have the student give short answers. For example:

T: Where is your grandfather living?

S: He's living in Beijing.

T: Who is he living with?

S: My father and mother.

T: Why is he living with them?

S: Because my father is his oldest son.

T: How is your grandfather doing?

S: Fine. His health is good.

T: What is he probably doing right now?

S: He's probably sleeping. It's 3 A.M. in Beijing.

- Have the class ask you similar questions about a relative of yours.

Note 2   *(Exercises 2–3)*

- To practice subject-pattern questions with *who*, ask about students' relatives and friends in different time zones. Have students explain their answers. Ask questions like the following:

T: Who is sleeping now?

S1: My parents are sleeping now. They're in Paris.

T: Who is eating dinner?

S2: My brother is. He's living in New York.

T: Who is getting up?

S3: My cousin in Hawaii is getting up. It's morning there.

- Ask each student to write one subject-pattern question with *who*. Have students read their questions to the class, and call on individuals to answer.

Focused Practice (pages 125–126)

Exercise 2

date: an arrangement to meet a boyfriend or girlfriend

Exercise 5

A way to vary this activity is for students to read the questions and predict the intonation based on the grammar. Then they can listen to the audio and use it to check whether their predictions were correct.

Communication Practice (page 127)

Exercise 6

Have students look back at Exercise 5 and use the questions there to try to predict the answers to the questions in this exercise. Then they can listen to the audio and use it to check whether their predictions were correct.

Exercise 7

Bring in a photograph or find a picture on the Internet that you can use to model this activity. As an example, bring in a photo of Mt. Fuji in Japan. Tell the class: "People are speaking Japanese. I'm wearing warm clothes. I'm skiing. It's snowing. Where am I?" Then show the picture.

Further Practice

Put students in pairs and tell them to pretend they are best friends. One friend is in the United States. The other is in his or her home country. They have not seen each other in several months, but they talk on the phone often. They should role-play a conversation, asking and answering questions about what they are doing, who they're doing it with, etc. Remind students to use some of their new expressions, such as *super, come on, you're kidding, why don't you*.

The conversation should start as follows:

S1: Hello?

S2: Hi _____! Guess what I'm doing!

S1: What are you doing?

What's playing? Do a skimming exercise. Use the entertainment listings from your local newspaper. Prepare a list of questions that use the present progressive. For example:

- What movie is playing at the _____ theater?
- What movie is playing at _____ o'clock at _____ theater?
- Which band is playing at (name of club)?

- What is happening at (amusement park)?
- Who's singing at _____?

The reading activity can be done as a competition. The first student or pair of students to find all the correct answers is the winner.

 UNIT 17 Possessive Nouns; *This / That / These / Those*

Unit Overview

In Unit 17 students will learn:
- the use of apostrophes with singular and plural possessive nouns
- *this, that, these, those* as pronouns and adjectives
- comments with *That's*, e.g., *That's great.*

Grammar in Context (pages 131–132)

Comprehension Questions

- How does Mark look? *(sharp)*
- Who is Mark having dinner with? *(Kathy and her parents)*
- What's the occasion? *(Kathy's parents' anniversary)*
- What is Mark wearing? *(his brother's jacket; his roommate's tie, shoes, and suspenders)*

Words

- Ask the students questions about men's clothing. For example, ask the men:
  —Do you have a tie / a sports jacket?
  —When do you wear them?
  —How are slacks different from pants?
- Write different occasions or places on the board. Examples:
  —*the opera*
  —*a job interview*
  —*a dance club*
  —*a wedding*
  —*dinner with parents*
- Ask the male students what they wear on these occasions or when they go to these places. Ask the female students what they like men to wear.

Expressions

Explain each expression and give additional examples.

- *You look sharp* means that someone is wearing good, clean clothes.
- *You know* is a way of getting a listener's attention before saying something meaningful.
- *I guess* means *I think*; it's used when a person is not quite certain about something.
- *No kidding* is an expression of surprise. In this case, Mark is surprised but pleased that he looks like a doctor.

Working Together

- Introduce the activity by asking students about the cultural aspects of compliments in different countries. Be aware that customs can be very different from what we expect in North America. In some cultures, for example, if you compliment a person's possession, they will feel obliged to give you the object. Americans give many more compliments than people in most other cultures. The idea of complimenting children for doing a "good job," as Americans commonly do, is exceedingly odd to people in most countries. Ask students questions like the following:
  —When do you give compliments in your culture?
  —What "rules" should a visitor to your country know about?
  —Is it proper for women to compliment men?
- Model compliments by complimenting your students.
- Students can compliment one another in groups. You can also have students stand in a circle, and have each student compliment the person to his or her right (or left).

Grammar Presentation (pages 133–134)

Identify the Grammar

- *It's her <u>parents'</u> anniversary.*
- *It's my <u>brother's</u> jacket.*
- *Are <u>these</u> suspenders OK?*
- *Sure. They go well with <u>that</u> tie and <u>those</u> shoes.*
- *<u>That's</u> terrific.*

Grammar Charts

- Regarding the first chart, ask students to paraphrase each sentence in order to show its meaning. For example:
  —My sister has a car. It is red.
  —The actress has a name. It is Rosa.
- Ask students where we put the apostrophe if the subject is singular / if the subject is plural.
- The chart on pronouns and adjectives builds on information presented in Unit 2. Students will probably know these structures already. What's new is the use of *this, that, these,* and *those* as demonstrative adjectives in sentences like "That tie is Steve's. / Those keys are Steve's." Highlight or circle the apostrophe in *Steve's.* Ask students to paraphrase the sentences with the verb *belong,* that is, "The tie belongs to Steve. / Those keys belong to Steve."
- Regarding the third chart, ask students for the long form of *That's. (That is)* Then ask what *that* means. *(It refers to the previous statement or fact.)*

Grammar Notes

Note 1
- Walk around the room and point to objects that belong to students. Elicit phrases such as *Hea-Jin's pencil, Dalia's purse,* etc.
- If further practice is needed, or instead of the above, collect objects from students and put them in a bag or box. Walk around the room and have students reach into the bag and pull out an object. The class says whose it is.

Note 2   *(Exercises 2–4)*
- Repeat one of the activities from Note 1, but this time do it as a dictation. Students first say who the object belongs to. Then they write the phrase. Do four or five phrases, then call students up to the board to write the phrases. Check for correct placement of the apostrophe. (All will be singular.)
- Dictate four or five plural phrases. Again, put the phrases on the board and correct them.
- Do a mix of singular and plural phrases. Have students write them on the board and ask students if each item is spelled correctly.

Note 3   *(Exercise 2)*
- Model several sentences with *this / that / these / those* + adjectives, e.g:
  —This window is open.
  —That light is broken.

—These keys are heavy.
—Those shoes are cool.
Stand next to the thing referred to by the noun when you use *this / these.* Stand farther back and point when you use *that / those.*
- Walk around the room. Stand next to items or pick them up. Call on students to form sentences with *this / these* + adjective. Stand back and point to elicit sentences with *that / those.*

Note 4   *(Exercise 4)*
- Write the following expressions on the board:
  —*That's nice.*
  —*That's great.*
  —*That's too bad.*
  —*That's awful.*
- Make a series of statements and instruct students to respond appropriately with one of the expressions on the board. For example:

T: My sister had a baby boy.

Ss: That's great.

Focused Practice (pages 134–137)

Exercise 1
repair: something you do to fix something that is broken or damaged

brake: the part of a bicycle, car, etc., that you use to slow or stop it

Exercise 2
steak: a thick, flat piece of meat

melt in your mouth: an expression meaning that a food is very tender

Exercise 4
impossible: here = behaving in an unreasonable and annoying way

Communication Practice (pages 137–138)

Exercise 7
The details of the passage may be confusing or difficult to remember. Play the audio as many times as necessary.

Exercise 8
Part A This activity can be done as a competition. Put students in groups and give them a time limit. The group that finds the most differences wins.

Part B Here is a variation of this activity which involves the whole class:

- Divide the class in half. Instruct half of the students to put several personal items on their desks. Include wearable items and some plural objects such as keys.
- Send the owners of the objects out of the room. While they are outside, the students remaining in the room "steal" their classmates' objects. They put on the wearable items and carry the others visibly.
- Call the first group back into the room. Their task is to find and collect their possessions. However, in order to reclaim an item, they must first make a sentence with *this, these, that,* or *those*. For example: "That's my hat. / Those are my keys."

Exercise 9

Call on several pairs of students to read each short conversation out loud.

Further Practice

Have students choose one of the following topics and write a paragraph. They may use the paragraphs in the chapter as models.

- Women's last names in their culture (Exercise 3, page 136)
- My Family's Favorite Foods (Exercise 6, page 137)

 **OUT OF THE BOX . . . . . .**

Telepathy.[1] In this activity, a student acting as your assistant will use "telepathy" to guess the identity of an object that the class selects while the assistant is out of the room. The procedure is as follows: At the beginning of the class, choose your "assistant" and send him or her out of the room. Have the class choose an object belonging to someone in the class, e.g., *Peter's jacket*. Tell students to concentrate hard on the object in order to send your assistant a "message" about the object. Call your assistant back into the room. Ask your assistant a series of questions about the object. The assistant should pretend to concentrate very hard before answering. For example:

T: Is it Melinda's backpack?

A: No.

T: Is it the television?

A: No.

T: Is it Vivian's iPod?

A: No.

Only you and your assistant know the secret: You will ask about something black (blue, red, etc.) just before the correct object. Thus, after asking about seven or eight incorrect objects, ask about something black. Your assistant will know that the *next* object is the one the class chose. Play the game once or twice more. Ask the class to guess how you did it. If they can't guess, tell them.

 UNIT 18

Count and Non-count Nouns; *Some* and *Any*

Unit Overview

In Unit 18 students will learn about count and non-count nouns, *some* and *any*, and quantifiers such as *a bowl of, a cup of*, etc.

Grammar in Context (pages 139–140)

Comprehension Questions

- What is Jessica Olson doing? *(interviewing people)*
- What is she asking them about? *(their eating habits)*
- What does the man eat for breakfast? *(a bagel and coffee)*
- What does the first woman have for breakfast? *(nothing at all)*
- What does the second woman have for breakfast? *(a bowl of cereal, some yogurt with fruit, and a glass of juice)*

Words

- Tell students what you eat and drink (or don't eat and drink) for breakfast, using some of the new words.
- Ask students what they eat. Use the new words in questions like the following:
  —Do you ever eat a bagel for breakfast?
  —Do you drink a cup of coffee before you leave for school?
  —Do you eat fruit for breakfast?
  —Who eats a sandwich for lunch?

---

[1] Source: Andrew Wright et al., *Games for Language Learning.* Cambridge: Cambridge University Press, 1983.

Expressions

- Explain that the phrase *Nothing at all?* is an expression of surprise. To elicit, ask the class: How does Speaker B feel? Follow up by asking the class if it is healthy to eat *nothing at all* for breakfast.
- If it is culturally appropriate, ask students to raise their hands if they are on a diet. Ask a student who raises his or her hand, "What do you eat every day?" After that student answers, go to the next student and ask, "What about you?" Repeat with all those who raised their hands.
- If no one is on a diet, ask the class if they know someone who is on a diet and what that person eats. Try to elicit *nothing at all*.
- People can also be *on a diet* to gain weight or muscle, for example, if they are in training for a sport. Ask the class who works out (exercises) regularly. Ask if they are on a special diet and what they eat.

Working Together

Part B
Ask several students to share their answers with the class.

Part C
- If necessary, draw pictures of or describe broccoli and cauliflower.
- After students guess the answer, ask:
  —Do you like the vegetables in this salad?
  —Which vegetables do you like to put in a salad?

Grammar Presentation (pages 141–142)

Identify the Grammar

- *I usually have <u>a bowl of cereal</u> and <u>some yogurt</u> with <u>fruit</u>—<u>a banana</u>, <u>a peach</u>, or <u>an orange</u>, or <u>some strawberries</u>.*
- *Do you have <u>any juice</u>?*

Grammar Charts

- Write the examples on the board.
- Help students to understand the differences between things we can count and things we cannot count. Say *a banana, a peach, an orange*. Ask:
  —How many bananas? How many peaches? How many oranges *(one in each case)*
  —What does *a / an* mean? *(one)*

—Can we count bananas, peaches, and oranges? *(yes)*
- Say *a banana*. Ask: *Does* banana *start with a vowel or a consonant? (consonant)*. Do the same for *a peach, an orange*. Then ask:
  —When do we say *a*? *(before a consonant)*
  —When do we say *an*? *(before a vowel)*
- Say *some strawberries*. Ask:
  —Can we count strawberries? *(yes)*
  —How do we make a noun plural? *(add -s or -es)*
  —Can we use *a / an* with plural nouns? *(no)*
  —What does *some* mean? *(more than one, but we don't know exactly how many)*
- Ask questions about the non-count nouns. Help students to understand that we can talk about limited quantities of non-count nouns by specifying the container that the noun comes in. Be aware of cultural differences, however; for example, some people drink coffee in a bowl. Ask:
  —Can we count cereal? Yogurt? Fruit? *(no; but be prepared to explain that for some English speakers, fruit is countable, e.g., "Would you like a fruit?")*
  —Can we use *some* with non-count nouns? *(yes)*
  —Can you think of other phrases similar to *a bowl of*? *(a cup of, a glass of, a box of, etc.)*
- Say *juice*. Ask:
  —What kind of noun is *juice*? *(non-count)*
  —Is it correct to say *I have any juice*? *(no)*
  —Is it correct to say *I don't have any juice*? *(yes)*
  —How do we use *any*? *(in negative statements and questions)*

Grammar Notes

Note 1

- Elicit a few more examples of countable foods. Write the examples on the board.
- Ask the class to say the plural of the nouns on the board. Write the plurals alongside the singular forms.
- Ask students if they remember the rules for adding *-s* versus *-es*. If not, refer back to Unit 4, Grammar Note 5, page 28, and Appendix 6, page A-6.)

Note 2 *(Exercise 2)*

- Write the following quantifiers on the board:
  —a bowl of   —a glass of
  —a slice of   —a cup of
  —a bottle of

- Ask students to give examples of non-count nouns with each quantifier. Write them on the board. Examples:
  —*a bowl of: cereal, salad, yogurt, ice cream, soup*
  —*a slice of: bread, cake, pizza*
  —*a bottle of: water, soda, juice*
  —*a glass of: water, tea, juice, soda, milk*
  —*a cup of: coffee, tea, hot chocolate*
- Elicit additional examples of non-count foods. (If students need help, tell them to think of foods they eat every day.) Write the foods and their quantifiers on the board, e.g., *a piece of fruit.*

Note 3
Have students make sentences using the non-count nouns already on the board. Elicit sentences with the verb *be* as well as other verbs, for example: "Coffee makes me nervous. / Ice cream has a lot of calories." Monitor students' sentences for correct use of the singular verb.

Note 4   *(Exercise 2)*
- Recast the grammar in the form of a diagram, like this:

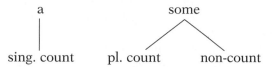

- Put students in pairs. Give each student one of the recipes below. Students should dictate their recipes to each other, taking care to use *a* and *an* correctly. They can begin as follows: "I want to tell you how to make a summer fruit salad. You will need a peach, two plums . . ."

Summer fruit salad for 2	Winter fruit salad for 2
1 peach	1 apple
2 plums	1 orange
1 banana	1 pear
1 apricot	1/2 can pineapple chunks
grapes	pineapple juice
melon pieces	grapefruit pieces
coconut	walnuts

- After listening, students should compare what they wrote with their partner's recipe.

Note 5   *(Exercise 3)*
- Recast the information as a diagram, like this:

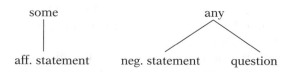

- Model a few more examples. If students brought their lunch to school, ask questions with *any* about their lunch contents. Elicit answers using *some / any*. For example:

T: Do you have any fruit today?

S: No, I don't have any fruit today. / Yes, I have some fruit today.

- Put students in groups of four for a game. Use the chart below or make one like it. Cut it into strips so that each student has a list of what he or she has and what he or she wants.

Student	1	2	3	4
You have	yogurt bread roast beef olives	coffee mineral water chicken milk	eggs spaghetti iced tea straw-berries	apples peanut butter chips ketchup
You want	milk straw-berries peanut butter	yogurt eggs apples	bread mineral water ketchup	olives coffee spaghetti

- Students should take turns asking and answering questions with this pattern:

A: Do you have any _____?

B: Yes, I have some _____. / No, I don't have any _____.

- If the first person a student asks has the item he or she wants, the questioner checks off that item on his or her "You want" list. The first student to check off all the items is the winner.

Note 6   *(Exercise 2)*
- Model the following sentence: *I like oranges, but I don't like grapefruit.*
- Instruct each student to make a similar sentence. Encourage students to use names of foods that have not yet been mentioned in the lesson.
- Go around the room and have students say their sentences.
- Follow up by naming students and asking the class to recall what they like and dislike.

→ For additional practice, see the Supplementary Activities on page 91.

Focused Practice (pages 143–145)

Exercise 1

meal: the food that you eat at one time, or the time it is eaten (e.g., breakfast, lunch, dinner)

cracker: a thin, hard, dry piece of bread with salt on it

roast beef: meat from a cow cooked in an oven

occasionally: sometimes but not often

once in a while: sometimes

hungry: wanting or needing to eat

Exercise 2

certainly: of course

Exercise 3

olive: a small green or black fruit eaten as food or used for making oil

Communication Practice (page 145)

Exercise 5

- To introduce the listening, ask students to read the title. If necessary, explain that *I can't believe . . .* can be an expression of disapproval. Model one or two examples, e.g., *I can't believe these prices!*
- Have students read the questions before listening. You may need to define *salsa* (a sauce made from onions, tomatoes, and hot-tasting peppers that you put on Mexican food) and *out of* (having none of something that you had before).
- Expand the activity by having students listen for singular, plural, and non-count nouns and placing them in a chart like the one in Exercise 1. For example:

Singular	Plural	Non-count
a snack	chips	lunch

Exercise 6

- This activity may be done as an interview. Put students in pairs. Have them interview each other and take notes on their partner's answers in a chart like this:

Likes	Dislikes
1.	1.
2.	2.
3.	3.

- The interviewer can say: "Tell me three kinds of food you like and three kinds of food you dislike."
- Now put two pairs of students together. Each student tells about his or her partner's answers. The new partners ask questions. For example:

S1: Tegum likes olives, chocolate, and apples. He doesn't like broccoli, milk, or hamburgers.

S2: Tegum, do you like red apples, yellow apples, or green apples?

Tegum: I like red apples.

Further Practice

Play a memory game. Have students sit in a circle. Sit with them. Begin the game by saying, for example: "I'm very hungry. I want to eat a piece of chicken." The student sitting to your right should repeat what you said and add an item, e.g., "I'm very hungry. I want to eat a piece of chicken and an apple." Continue around the circle, with each speaker repeating what all the previous speakers said and then adding one item. Students are "in" the game as long as they can remember all the items mentioned. The are "out" if they forget an item.

 GRAMMAR OUT OF THE BOX . . . . . .

Recipes. Students will tell the class how to prepare a simple food or drink. To prepare, show students the model below. Go over the recipe with them. Then give them a blank version and have them fill it out. Help them with vocabulary as needed.

Recipe Worksheet

Garlic Salad Dressing

Ingredients:

   6 tablespoons olive oil

   3 tablespoons red wine vinegar or lemon juice

   1 tablespoon water

   1 clove garlic

   salt

   pepper

Steps:

   1. Crush the garlic with a garlic press. Put the crushed garlic in a jar.

   2. Measure the oil, vinegar, and water and put them in the jar.

---

3. Add some salt and pepper according to your taste.
4. Add a tiny amount of powdered oregano if you like.
5. Close the jar and shake.
6. Pour immediately on fresh salad.

Provide a scaffold for the students' oral presentation. For example: "I want to tell you how to make my favorite salad dressing. You will need 6 tablespoons of olive oil . . . First, crush the garlic. . . . Second, . . . Third, . . . Finally, . . . I hope you will enjoy this easy and delicious recipe." Have students practice once with a partner. Circulate as they are practicing and help with vocabulary, pronunciation, etc. Have students take turns telling the class their recipes. Leave time for listeners to ask questions.

Follow up with a class potluck. You may want to collect the written recipes and make a class recipe book.

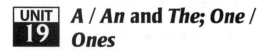

UNIT 19 *A / An* and *The; One / Ones*

Unit Overview

In Unit 19 students will learn when to use *a / an* or *the*. They will also learn how to replace a noun with *one* or *ones*.

Grammar in Context (pages 146–147)

Comprehension Questions

• Where are the speakers? *(in a clothing store)*
• What is Ken looking for? *(a sports jacket)*
• Which jacket does Ken like? *(the blue one)*
• Does Laura like it? *(no)*

Words

• Ask questions and use objects in the room to help students understand the words. For example, point to students' clothing items and ask, "Is the color bright or dull?" Or ask, in general, "Which colors are bright? / Which ones are dull?"
• Elicit examples of formal and casual clothing for men and women. For example, a sports jacket is casual, but a suit is formal. For women, a business suit is formal, but jeans are casual.

• Ask students if they buy things on sale. For contrast, you may need to use the phrase *full price*. Talk about stores that have good sales or times of the year when there are good sales (e.g., after Christmas, Thanksgiving weekend).
• Ask students, "Do you always try on clothes before you buy them?" This is not an odd question in the United States, where most stores allow you to return items you have bought. Some people buy many items, try them on at home, and then return the ones they don't want. Other people try on clothes in the *dressing room / fitting room* of the store. Ask students what they usually do.
• Tell the class your shoe size, e.g., "My shoe size is 9." Then ask several students to say their shoe sizes. Sum up by saying, e.g., "We have different shoe sizes."

Expressions

Write all the new expressions on the board. Then say sentences like the following and have students respond with an appropriate expression. (There may be more than one acceptable response.)
• Do you have this jacket in size 10? *(You're in luck.)*
• Here's the jacket in size 10. *(Can I try it on?)*
• Can you bring me this jacket in a different size? *(Sure. Be right back.)*
• Should I buy this sweater? *(It's up to you.)*
• I'd like to pay with a credit card. *(It's up to you.)*

Working Together

Part B
• Do the activity in the book with the whole class. Monitor for the correct use of *one / ones*.
• Expand by bringing in pairs of real foods or objects. Clothes from your own wardrobe would be entertaining as well.

Grammar Presentation (pages 148–149)

Identify the Grammar

• *We're having <u>a</u> sale.*
• *I have <u>an</u> interview.*
• *I really like <u>the</u> blue <u>one</u>.*
• *All <u>the</u> black <u>ones</u> are dull.*

Grammar Charts

- Write the example sentences on the board.
- Review the use of singular and plural count nouns. Point to the nouns in the first two sentences on the board and ask:
  —When do we use *a*? *(before a singular count noun that begins with a consonant)*
  —When do we use *an*? *(before a singular count noun that begins with a vowel)*
  —How do we form plural nouns? *(with -s or -es)*
  —How do we speak about items in general? *(by using the plural)*
- Point to the third sentence. First ask the class, "What does *one* mean?" *(sports jacket).* Explain that *one* is a pronoun. It replaces a noun. Point to the last sentence and ask similar questions regarding *ones*. *(Ones refers to all the black jackets.)*
- Now focus students' attention on the use of *the*. They already know that *one / ones* refers to jackets. Now point to *the* and ask, "Which suit / suits?" *(the blue suit / the black suits)* Tell students that we use *the* when we know which one or ones.

Grammar Notes

Note 1   *(Exercises 2–3)*
This note repeats information presented in the previous chapter. To review, write a few sentences with errors on the board. Then have students find the errors and state the rule. For example:
- *I'm doing a homework.*
- *I'd like a apple.*
- *He's student at an university.* (Note: Trick question! There are two errors. Students may not know that we use *a* before words starting with the letter *u* pronounced like /yu/.)
- *I want to buy an necklace.*

Note 2   *(Exercise 3)*
- This note addresses both the meaning and use of *the*. It may take a great deal of practice before students understand the concept of "specific things that the speaker and listener know about." It is helpful to return to the question *Which one / ones?* If both the speaker and the listener know which one / ones, <u>and each speaker knows that the other one also knows</u>, then they use *the*. In the example given here, ask the class, "Why do the salesperson and customer use *the*?" *(Both of them know which suits they're talking about because they can see them.)*

- Provide a few more examples.
  —Ask a student to get up and walk to *the door*. Then tell the student to open *the door*. Ask the class, "Why did I say *the door*?" *(Everybody knows which door because we can see it and because the room has only one door.)*
  —Pick up a marker or other teaching tool, lay it down somewhere, and then pretend you forgot where it is. Look around while saying, "Where's the marker?" Then ask the class why you said *the*. Elicit "We can see it." Also, the students know about the marker because they've seen you use it before.
- To reinforce the rule about the use of *the*, bring in any short text. Make copies and have students circle all appearances of *the*. Then have them note which type of noun comes after: singular, plural, or non-count.

Note 3   *(Exercise 3)*
- Elicit similar nouns that take *the* because there is only one of that item. Write the following contexts on the board. Then elicit examples from the students and write them on the board:

Nature / the universe	Your home	Your school or classroom
the moon, the stars, the equator[1]	the dog, the refrigerator, the garage, the bathroom, the couch	the teacher, the office, the elevator, the board

- You may wish to put students in groups and assign one of the above contexts to each group. Students come up with examples in their groups and then share with the whole class.

Note 4   *(Exercise 3)*
- Model a few more examples like the one in the book. For example: "I bought a loaf of bread and some fish. The fish was on sale for $3.99 a pound."
- Make statements with *a*. Have students make a follow-up comment with *the*. For example:

T: This building has an elevator.

Ss: The elevator is slow.

---

[1] If students provide incorrect examples such as "the Mars," "the Africa," briefly explain that we usually don't use articles with names in English. Exceptions are places such as the North Pole, which has the structure of *the* + adjective + noun.

Note 5

- A fun way to practice this point is to bring in candies of different colors, such as M & Ms. (You can also use other multi-colored, similar objects.) Place candies of different colors on a plate or tray and walk around the room. Offer the tray to students, who say, "I'd like a _____ one." Then the student takes the candy.
- To practice the plural, repeat the activity, but when students say, "I'd like the _____ ones," they should take all the candies of that color.

Focused Practice (pages 149–151)

Exercise 2
novel: a book that tells a long story about someone or something

umbrella: a piece of cloth or plastic stretched over a frame that you can hold over your head to protect yourself from the rain

Exercise 3
else: more

dress shoes: formal shoes

Communication Practice (pages 151–152)

Exercise 5
Have students read the title and predict who is speaking and what they are speaking about. Then have them read the questions before listening.

Exercise 6
Expand by collecting pairs of similar objects from the students. Lay the pairs on your desk. Then have students form sentences like the ones in the book, saying which items they like and giving a reason.

Exercise 7
The exercise title asks, "What's wrong with this picture?" After students have worked in groups, have them write sentences that answer the question on the board. Call on different students to read the sentences and correct any errors.

Further Practice
Have students role-play a conversation similar to the one in the opening reading. Put students in groups of three. Two students are friends shopping together and the third is a salesperson. To prepare, the "friends" should decide who and what they are shopping for.

They should pick the size, color, and style they want. The "salesperson" should not hear this conversation. Now the students should come together for the role play. The salesperson should offer to help and bring the friends several of the desired items to choose from. At the end of the conversation, one of the friends should choose an item to buy. The speakers should use articles and *one / ones* in their conversation. If there is time, have each group perform their role play in front of the class. If time is limited, put two groups together and have them take turns performing for one another.

Special occasion. Students will choose clothes for a special occasion, such as a Christmas party, formal dance, wedding, etc. Bring in a variety of clothing catalogues for both men and women. Try to have one catalogue for every three or four students. Explain the task. Tell the students you are hosting some kind of special event and they are all invited. Unfortunately, several students in the class don't have the right clothes, so their classmates need to help them shop for the event. Put students in groups. One person in each group should be the one that the others are shopping for. The students should look through the catalogues together and select a complete outfit, including shoes and jewelry, if appropriate, for their classmate. Model the language students will need and write it on the board. For example:

- *Here are some suits. I think this one will look good on you, Han.*
- *Do you like this one or that one?*
- *This one is nice.*
- *The red ones are good for you.*

When time is up, have each group show the class the outfit they selected for their classmate.

 UNIT 20 *Can / Can't*

Unit Overview

In Unit 20 students will learn the use of *can* and *can't* to express ability, possibility, and requests.

Grammar in Context (pages 153–154)

Comprehension Questions

- What is Kathy's message to Mark? *(I can't meet you today.)*
- What is the problem with Kathy's message? *(Mark can't understand all the numbers.)*
- Does Kathy have her cell phone? *(no)*
- Where is Mark going? *(to take a package to the Daily Times)*
- Is Steve worried about Kathy? *(no)*

Words

- Ask students to raise their hands if they have cell phones. Ask a few students, e.g., "What is your phone number?"
- Ask students to raise their hands if they have an answering machine. Ask:
  —How many phone messages do you usually get in a day?
  —When you call a friend and get an answering machine, do you usually leave a message?

Expressions

- Ask the class why, in the conversation, Mark says "Thanks for coming" to Judy and Steve. *(He called and asked them to come over because he needed their help.)* Ask the class about other situations in which a person might use this phrase *(e.g., when someone drops by their home or work).*
- Ask a few students to do you a favor. For example, ask them to open the window, bring you a book, erase the board, etc. Try to make the requests genuine. Have students respond to each request with *Of course* or *No problem.*
- Try to get students to explain *in trouble.* Ask them: "Where is Kathy? What's the problem?" Elicit examples of *in trouble:* "She had a car accident. / She's sick." (Note: *She's late* is not a good example of *in trouble.*)
- Ask students for the meaning of *take it easy* (relax). Ask, "When do we say this?" *(when we want to help a person calm down)*

Working Together

Part B
Only the last digit of Kathy's phone number was unclear, so Steve and Judy can try dialing the number with a different last digit until they get the right one. They can also wait for Kathy to call.

Grammar Presentation (page 155)

Identify the Grammar

- *I <u>can't meet</u> you today.*
- *<u>Can</u> you <u>hear</u> the last number?*
- *No, I <u>can't</u>.*
- *<u>Where can</u> she <u>be</u>?*
- *Judy and I <u>can get</u> her phone number.*

Grammar Charts

Write the examples on the board and ask questions like the following to help students notice the grammar:
- Which form of the verb do we use after *can* and *can't*? *(the base form)*
- Do we use *to* with *can* and *can't*? *(no)*
- What is the word order in *yes / no* questions? *(Can + subject + verb)*
- What is the word order in *wh-* questions? *(Wh- word + can + subject + verb)*

Grammar Notes

Note 1 *(Exercise 2)*
- On the board, create a chart like the following:

Ability	Possibility	Request

- Point to each category and give a few examples of each; paraphrase the meanings of *can / can't*, e.g.:
  —Ability: I can cook Italian food. I can swim. / I know how to do these things.
  —Possibility: I can wait for you. / It's possible for me to do this.
  —Request: Can you help me? Can you do me a favor? / I need help.
- Put students in groups and give them a list of sentences like the following. They should decide on the meaning of each sentence.

1. Jasmine can speak French. *(ability)*
2. Mr. Ross can see you tomorrow at 3 P.M. *(possibility)*
3. Can you please open the window? *(request)*
4. Mark can't meet Kathy for lunch. He's busy. *(not possible)*
5. We can't go skiing because there isn't any snow. *(lack of ability)*

6. People can't fly, but some birds can talk. *(lack of ability / ability)*
7. Can someone erase the board, please? *(request)*
8. In San Francisco we can stay with Judy's brother. *(possibility)*

• Call students up to the board and have them write the numbers of the sentences in the correct columns on the chart.

Note 2 *(Exercise 2)*
• Say three or four sentences about things you can do very well. Be sure to model correct pronunciation. Examples:
—I can speak French.
—I can sing.
—I can make chicken soup.
• Ask the class: "How about you?" Then go around the room in a chain and have each student say one thing he or she does well.

Note 3 *(Exercise 2)*
Repeat the procedure from Note 1, but have students form negative sentences.

Note 4
• To elicit questions about abilities, write the following on the board:
—*What can he do?*
—*Can he (shake hands)?*
• Tell the class that you have a truly amazing dog (parrot, cat, etc.) Repeat that this dog is truly remarkable; he can do things that no other dog can do. Then point to the board. Students should get the idea that they are supposed to ask you questions. Elicit, for example: "What can he do? / Can your dog roll over, sit, lie down, open the door, bring you the newspaper?" Answer the students' questions and then ask them if they agree that this is truly a fantastic animal.
• Repeat with students coming forward to answer questions about their "amazing" pets.
• To have students practice asking for favors, give each student an index card. Instruct them to write on the card an item they need or something they need someone to do for them, e.g., a dictionary, a ride home.
• On the board, write: *Of course. / Sure. / No problem. / Sorry, I can't.*
• Collect the cards and put them in a box or hat. To model, draw a card. Choose a student and ask, "Can you do me a favor? Can you (wash my car / do my homework / give me a dollar)?" The student you chose should respond using one of the phrases on the board.

• Repeat by walking around the room, having students draw cards, asking for favors, etc.

Focused Practice (pages 156–157)

Exercise 1
uh-huh: (informal) used to say yes or that you understand something

Exercise 2
Mandarin: the official language of China

look up: to find a piece of information in a reference book, on a computer, etc.

on the way: to be arriving soon

Exercise 3
ice skater: a person who knows how to move across ice wearing special shoes

Communication Practice (pages 158–159)

Exercise 4
Follow up by having pairs of students read the sentences with correct stress.

Exercise 5
A variation of the instructions in the book would be to have pairs of students swap papers with another pair. In other words, each pair of students would read the sentences written by another pair.

Exercise 6
• Have one student from each group write that group's list on the board. If you want, you can change the game rules so that a group only gets a point for an item that no other group has.
• Say, and have students repeat, the items on the board.

Exercise 7
Students should sit down when they have three names. Go around the room and have each student make one sentence, e.g., "Kim can play chess. / Dion can change a tire. / Han-suk can water ski."

Further Practice
Bring in simple items or pictures of items. Divide students into groups of three or four. Display all the items for the whole class to see, or give one item to each group. The students' task is to make a list of both ordinary and

unusual things they can do with this item. For example:

Pencil—You can:
• write with it
• erase
• scratch your head (back, etc.)
• stir your coffee
• chew it
• carve on it
• throw it

Give a time limit of five minutes. After the groups finish talking, have them share their ideas with another group or with the whole class.

GRAMMAR OUT OF THE BOX......

Interview. Make two handouts with different lists of six to eight verbs and two blank lines, like the following; explain that students should think of their own items and write them on the blank lines.

Student 1	Student 2
swim	ski
whistle	play piano
touch your toes without bending your knees	speak Chinese
cook spaghetti	stay up all night
sleep on an airplane	drive a motorcycle
_____	_____
_____	_____

Demonstrate the activity with a student. Ask, "Can you swim / whistle," etc.? If the student answers yes, place a check next to the verb. Put students in pairs and give each partner a different paper. Have them use their verbs to interview one another. They should answer truthfully. For example:

S1: Can you swim?

S2: Yes, I can. Can you ski?

As a follow-up, go around the room and call on each student to make a sentence about his or her partner, as follows: "Aki can swim, but she can't whistle."

UNIT 21 The Simple Past: Regular Verbs (Statements)

Unit Overview

In Unit 21 students will learn the use of the simple past of regular verbs in affirmative and negative statements.

Grammar in Context (pages 163–164)

Comprehension Questions

• Where is Kathy? What is she doing? *(She's attending a convention in Boston.)*
• Does Kathy like Boston? *(yes)*
• Did she enjoy the convention? Why? *(No, because she was too busy.)*
• Who is Ted? *(Kathy's cousin)*

Words

• Ask students for the names of some hotels in your town, or ask them for the name and location of their favorite hotel.
• Have students look at the drawing and tell you what a convention is. *(a large, formal meeting of people who belong to the same profession, organization, etc., or who have similar interests)* Ask the class who has a job. Ask those who raise their hands, "Do you sometimes go to a convention for your job?"
• Ask students to look at the picture of a presentation. Ask, "What is happening in the picture?" *(A woman is talking.)* "Where is she talking?" (Elicit: *at a conference*).
• If you have attended a convention and presented a talk there, tell the class about your experience.

Expressions

Have students read all items and ask questions to help them understand the meaning and use of the expressions. For example:

• For item 1, ask students: "Did you go to a party last weekend? Was it a blast?" Paraphrase if necessary, e.g., "Did you enjoy it?"
• For item 2, ask: "How was the movie?" *(great)* Then ask students to explain the meaning of *another story.* (In other words, the restaurant was bad.)

- Ask students to read item 3 and ask:
  —How does the speaker feel? *(happy)*
  —When do English speakers say *thank goodness*? *(when they're happy or thankful)*
- For item 4, ask: "How does Speaker B feel?" *(happy, excited, enthusiastic)*

Working Together

Part B
Extend by having students tell a parallel story using the same verbs but different nouns. For example: "A woman attended a doctors' convention in Bangkok, Thailand. She stayed at the Empire Hotel. She listened to a presentation about new medicine for headaches."

Grammar Presentation (pages 165–166)

Identify the Grammar
- *Everyone <u>enjoyed</u> them.*
- *We all <u>missed</u> you.*
- *I <u>arrived</u> here late Monday night.*
- *I <u>didn't finish</u> until 9:00 at night.*

Grammar Charts

Ask questions like the following to help students infer the structure of the simple past:

- How do we form the affirmative past of regular verbs? *(by adding -ed)*
- How do we form the negative? *(didn't + base form)*
- Which time expressions can we use with the simple past? *(yesterday, ago, last)*
- Today is (date). What was the date two days ago? *(Answers will vary.)*

Grammar Notes

Note 1   *(Exercises 2–3)*
- Do a drill on the complete conjugation of the simple past affirmative form. Choose a verb, e.g., *walk*. Say the pronouns *I, you, he, she, it, we, you, they*. Have students repeat the pronoun and add the past form of the verb.
- Ask, "Does the form of the past tense change from singular to plural?" *(no)* "Is it the same for all persons?" *(yes)*

Note 2   *(Exercises 2–3)*
Write the following list of verbs on the board. Put students in pairs and small groups and instruct them to add *-d* or *-ed*. Refer students back to the rule in the book if they make mistakes.

move	*travel*	*love*
marry	*enjoy*	*open*
dream	*receive*	*agree*

Note 3   *(Exercise 3)*
- Drill the conjugation as you did for Note 1.
- Model the pronunciation of *didn't* with several verbs.
- Drill by saying the uncontracted form of several verbs, and have students restate using the contracted form. For example:

T: He did not eat.

Ss: He didn't eat.

- Do a transformation drill from affirmative to negative and vice versa, as follows:
  —T: I talked to my mother.
    Ss: I didn't talk to my mother.
  —T: Tomas called a friend.
    Ss: Tomas didn't call a friend.
  —T: We didn't watch a movie.
    Ss: We watched a movie.
  —T: They didn't walk to work.
    Ss: They walked to work.

Note 4
- Put a two-column chart like the one below on the board or on an overhead transparency. Instruct students to compose sentences using the time expression you point to and one of the verbs on the right. Remind students to make some negative sentences.

Time expressions	Verbs

yesterday
yesterday morning / afternoon /
  evening
two days / a week / month /
  year / ago
last night / week / month / year
	enjoy, look, miss, arrive,
	work, start, finish, talk,
	attend, listen, stay, study,
	graduate, learn, agree,
	use, help, open, clean,
	play, rain, watch, love,
	receive, want, travel

- After a student makes a sentence, select another student to restate it with the time expression in a different position. For example:

—S1: I dreamed about my girlfriend last night.
  S2: Last night I dreamed about my girlfriend.
—S1: Last week I didn't clean my apartment.
  S2: I didn't clean my apartment last week.

Focused Practice (pages 166–168)

Exercise 1
hire: to pay someone to work for you

fire: to make someone leave his or her job

offer: to say that you are willing to do something

partners: the owners of a business

end up: to be in a particular situation that you did not intend or expect

Exercise 2
do well: to succeed

Exercise 4
speech: a talk given to a group of people

awesome: very impressive; extremely good

Communication Practice (pages 168–169)

Exercise 5
• A way to vary the listening activity is as follows: Play an item, then pause the tape. Before students fill in the blanks in the book, call on them to restate what they heard. Monitor their pronunciation of the simple past.
• As a follow-up, students can write alternative scripts to fit the incomplete sentences in the text. Then put them in pairs or groups, and have them dictate their scripts to one another.

Exercise 6
Part A
Note that there is only one correct way to fill in each blank. Students do not need to hear the sentences in order to do this step.
Part B
To ensure that students heard correctly, call a student up to the board. Have the class say each verb. The student points to the column indicating the pronunciation.

Exercise 7
• Instruct students to include at least one negative sentence among the four they compose.
• As a follow-up with the whole class, call the name of each student in turn. Have each student's group members repeat the true

sentences about him or her. Monitor each speaker for correct pronunciation.

Exercise 8
Expand by adding more verbs for students to use. Below is a bank of regular verbs that appear in this chapter.

> enjoy, look, miss, arrive, work, start, finish, talk, attend, listen, stay, study, graduate, hire, fire, learn, offer, agree, end up, use, help, open, clean, play, rain, watch, love, receive, want, travel

Further Practice
Play a game called "Past Pronunciation Bingo."
Preparation
Make Bingo cards with nine boxes. In each box, write /t/, /d/, or /ɪd/. Vary the order from card to card. (Note: There should be many more /t/ and /d/ than /ɪd/ endings.) For example:

/ɪd/	/t/	/d/
/d/	/t/	/t/
/t/	/d/	/ɪd/

Write each verb from the word bank in Exercise 8 on a separate slip of paper. Write the base form. Put all the slips in a hat or box.
Procedure
Give each student or pair of students a Bingo card. To play, pull a slip of paper out of the hat or box. (Note: You can also have a student or students do this.) Say the verb. Students must figure out how to pronounce the past of the verb and write the verb in one of the corresponding boxes on their card. For example, if the verb is *clean*, students would write this word in *one* (not all!) of the /d/ boxes on their cards As soon as a student has filled in three boxes in a row in any direction, he or she should call out "Bingo!" To check, have the student who called "Bingo!" say the verbs in their past forms.

What happened before? In this activity students tell what happened before the moment captured in a photo or picture. Prepare by collecting photos or pictures that lend themselves to imaginative storytelling. Magazine advertisements, funny personal photos, pictures showing the aftermath of a natural disaster, or cartoons all work well. In class, distribute the pictures, one to each student or pair of students. Tell students their task is to tell the story of what happened *immediately before* the scene shown in the picture. Encourage them to be imaginative and include details such as the place, time, day, etc., of the event. As students are writing their stories, circulate and help with vocabulary as needed. When students' stories are ready, have them come up in front of the class one by one, show their pictures, and tell their stories. (In large classes you can divide students into groups for this part of the activity.) A variation of this activity is for all the students in the class to look at the *same* picture and compose different versions of what happened just before.

The Simple Past: Regular and Irregular Verbs; *Yes / No* Questions

UNIT 22

Unit Overview

In Unit 22 students will learn:
• statements with irregular past verbs
• past *yes / no* questions
• short answers

Grammar in Context (pages 170–171)

Background Note

In the conversation, Amanda says that she and Josh had an *adventure*. One definition of *adventure* is "an exciting thing that happens to someone."

Comprehension Questions

• Where did Amanda and Josh go? *(out of town)*
• What time did they leave? *(3 P.M.)*
• What happened at 4 o'clock? *(It started to snow.)*
• Did Amanda and Josh drive in the snow? *(No. They stopped.)*
• Did they call for help? *(No. Amanda's cell phone was dead.)*
• What did they eat? *(cookies and chocolate bars)*
• Was it cold? *(Yes; it was freezing.)*
• Did they sleep? *(not much)*

• What happened in the morning? *(A snowplow came and cleared the road.)*

Words

Demonstrate the new words with pantomimes or gestures. For example, the word *deep* can be illustrated by raising your hand above your head. *Dark* and *light* can be shown by turning on and off the lights in your classroom. To illustrate *put on*, pretend to put on pants, a shirt, etc. Paraphrase *during the night* with the words *from* and *to*, for example, "from 10 P.M. to 6 A.M." or "from dark to light."

Expressions

• Ask students about their experiences. For example, ask who stayed home last weekend and who went out of town.
• Pantomime a dead cell phone. You may wish to point out that the opposite is not a "live" cell phone but rather a *charged* phone.

Working Together

Instruct students to take turns asking and answering questions.

Grammar Presentation (pages 172–173)

Identify the Grammar
• We <u>had</u> an adventure.
• <u>Did</u> you <u>stop</u>?
• <u>Did</u> you <u>have</u> anything to eat?
• <u>Yes, we did</u>, actually.
• We <u>drank</u> it during the night.
• We <u>didn't sleep</u> much.

Grammar Charts

• Write the examples on the board. Have students look at them and at the examples in the first chart. For each irregular past verb, elicit the base form, e.g.: *ate—eat; had—have*. (Hint: If students don't know, they can find the base form by looking at the negative sentences.)
• For *yes / no* questions, ask students to write a "formula" showing the word order, i.e., *Did* + subject + verb.
• For the short answers, ask students if the form changes for singular vs. plural subjects. *(no)*

Grammar Notes

Notes 1 and 2 *(Exercise 2)*

- Review the affirmative and negative past forms of regular verbs. Do a transformation drill in which you say an affirmative sentence and students change it to the negative. They should use contractions. Choose from the following verbs: *study, look, arrive, work, finish, talk, rain, travel, help, learn, watch.* For example:

  T: I watched TV last night.

  Ss: I didn't watch TV last night.

- Now say negative sentences and have students change them to affirmative. Listen for correct pronunciation of the regular past ending. For example:

  T: The mail didn't arrive.

  Ss: The mail arrived.

Notes 3 and 4 *(Exercise 3)*

- Drill *yes / no* questions and short answers as follows: Prompt students with a verb phrase. Have one student form a question and another student answer. Ask a set of questions to which all the answers are *yes*, followed by a set to which all the answers are *no*. For example:

  Yes answer

  T: sleep well

  S1: Did you sleep well last night?

  S2: Yes, I did.

  No answer

  T: eat a hamburger

  S1: Did you eat a hamburger yesterday?

  S2: No, I didn't.

- Provide another set of cues, but this time students should answer truthfully, yes or no. For example:

  T: go to bed early

  S1: Did you go to bed early last night?

  S2: Yes, I did.

  S3: No, I didn't.

Note 5

- Say each past form and have the class repeat. (Note: In some languages *be born* is always said in the present. If necessary, point out that this is incorrect in English.)
- Put students in pairs. Have them take turns drilling each other on the past forms. S1 says the present form and S2 responds with the

past. Then they switch (S1 says the past, S2 responds with the present.)

→ For additional practice, see the Supplementary Activities on page 91.

Focused Practice (pages 173–175)

Exercise 1

starved: (informal) very hungry

scrambled eggs: eggs that have had their white and yellow parts mixed together and then cooked

Exercise 2

one of those days: a bad day (i.e., one of those days where everything goes wrong)

the shop: the car repair shop

Exercise 4

flight: a trip on a plane

Communication Practice (pages 175–176)

Exercise 5

- Before listening, have students tell what they know about Mt. Fuji. (It's the tallest mountain in Japan, located just west of Tokyo.) If your students are not Japanese and you have access to a map of Japan, have them find Mt. Fuji and the town of Hamamatsu.
- Have students read the questions before listening.

Exercise 6

- If your class is too large for students to mingle all at once, put them in pairs or groups for this activity.
- Another variation is to put students in groups of seven. Each student in the group asks one question and polls all the others. To extend, put two groups together and have each student report to the other group on the results of his or her poll.

Exercise 7

Remind students to use the list of irregular verbs in Appendix 11, page A-14.

Further Practice

By now students will be very familiar with the "Find Someone Who . . ." activity, so vary it by having them write their own questions. Put students in pairs and have them turn to the list of irregular verbs on page 179. Instruct them to write seven *yes / no* questions using the verbs and the past time expressions they learned in Unit 21. For example:

- Were you born in 1983?
- Did you sleep eight hours last night?
- Did you eat fruit yesterday?
- Did you get an A on the last test?

Have students circulate individually and ask their questions. They should write the name of a classmate who answers *yes* next to each question. Put students in groups and have them report on the answers they collected. For example: "Anwar was born in 1983. / Gina slept eight hours last night. / Corina ate fruit yesterday. / Stephan got an A on the last test."

Adventure stories. Have students tell real stories about unusual, dangerous, funny, exciting, or surprising experiences. Students may write an outline or the full text of their stories. Instruct them to use both regular and irregular past verbs. You may wish to provide a bank of verbs taken from Units 21 and 22. Teach students how to interrupt by saying *Excuse me* followed by a *yes / no* question. Tell the class about an adventure of your own, and instruct them to interrupt you and ask about the details of the story. Put students in small groups to tell their stories. Instruct listeners to interrupt with *yes / no* questions.

The Simple Past: *Wh-* Questions

Unit Overview

In Unit 23 students will learn:
- *Wh-* questions in the simple past
- Short answers to *wh-* questions
- More irregular verbs

Grammar in Context (pages 177–178)

Comprehension Questions

- Who called Amanda? *(her brother, Rob)*
- What happened to Rob? *(He had a car accident.)*
- How did it happen? *(He tried to park and hit a sign.)*

- How is Rob? *(fine)*
- What did Rob do to the car? *(He broke the headlights and dented the bumper.)*
- Where is Rob now? *(at a body shop)*

Words

- Model the pronunciation of the words and have students repeat.
- If possible, bring in a toy car or a picture of a car and point out the bumper and headlights. If students are interested, teach the name of other car parts as well.
- Ask the class who has had a car accident. If time permits, let one or two students tell about their experience.
- Inform students that an *auto repair shop* is often referred to simply as a *shop*. When someone's car is being repaired, the person may say that the car is *in the shop* or *at the garage.*

Expressions

- For the expression *It's for you,* pantomime picking up a ringing phone, answering, listening, and then passing the phone to another person while saying, "It's for you." This will serve to clarify the meaning of *it* in the phrase (i.e., the phone call).
- On the board, write *1. bad; 2. worse.* To illustrate, ask the class, "What's the first bad thing Rob did?" *(He had an accident.)* "What's the second bad thing? / What's worse?" *(He drove without Dad's OK).* Explain that *worse* means *more bad.*
- Model the intonation of *uh-oh.* Have students repeat. Ask, "When do we say *uh-oh*?" *(when we hear about an accident or bad new)* If necessary, provide a few other examples and have the class respond with *uh-oh.*
- Model the reduced pronunciation of *What do you mean,* i.e., *whaddaya mean.* Ask students why Amanda said this. *(She is surprised, she disagrees with Josh, or she wants clarification.)*

Working Together

- For Part A, call a student to the front to read Amanda's lines. You read Kathy's lines dramatically to show her concern.
- Assign parts of the conversation to different pairs of students, then have them come up before the class and do a "dramatic reading."

Grammar Presentation (page 179)

Identify the Grammar
- *When did it happen?*
- *Where did it happen?*
- *Why did you drive there?*

Wh- questions about the subject
- *What happened?*

Grammar Charts
- Write the example questions on the board.
- Have students look at the first three questions on the board and in the book. Ask the following questions:
  —What is the word order for these *wh-* questions *(wh- word + did + subject + verb)*
  —What form of the verb do we use? *(the base form)*
- Next, have students look at the subject-pattern questions. Ask:
  —What is the word order? *(wh- word + verb)*
  —How do we answer questions with *who*, e.g., "Who drove?" *(with the person's name or the name + did)*
- Say the irregular verbs and have students repeat. Then have them cover the chart. Say the base form and have them say the past.

Grammar Notes

Note 1   *(Exercises 2, 4)*
- Drill the form of most *wh-* questions by saying answers and having students ask questions according to your cues. Do 14 or 15 answer-and-question sets so that students can get in the habit. For example:

T: I went to a movie with Richard. / Who

Ss: Who did you go to a movie with?

T: The movie started at 8:30 P.M. / When

Ss: When did the movie start?

T: We ate dinner at home. / Where

Ss: Where did you eat dinner?

T: I stayed home last night. / Why

Ss: Why did you stay home?

- To enable students to ask genuine questions, say a simple sentence about something unusual you did or something that happened to you, e.g., "I bought flowers yesterday." Have students ask questions with *who, where,*

when, why, and answer them truthfully. For example:

S1: Why did you buy flowers?

T: It was my mother's birthday.

S2: Where did you buy them?

T: At the supermarket.

- Repeat the previous step, but this time call on a student to say what happened and answer the class's questions.

Note 2   *(Exercises 2–4)*
- Pick a student and tell the class that it was recently this person's birthday (wedding, anniversary, graduation, etc.), and he or she got a lot of wonderful gifts. The student wants to write thank-you notes to the people who gave the gifts, but unfortunately all the gift cards got mixed up. The student needs the class's help to figure out who gave which gift.
- Make a list of gifts and write each one on a slip of paper. Distribute the slips among the students.
- Using the gift list you prepared, model a few questions, e.g.:
  —Who gave John a baseball bat?[1]
  —Who bought John a poster of Green Day?
  —Who got him a bag of gourmet coffee?
- The classmate who "bought" each gift should respond with "I did."
- Give the list to the student you picked and have him or her continue asking questions, e.g., "Who bought me a wallet?"

Pronunciation Note
- Model additional pairs of sentences that have the same words but different stress and intonation. For example:
  —Where did you **eat**?
    Where did you eat?
  —Who did you **see**?
    Who did you see?
- Have students raise one finger if the speaker is asking for information. They should raise two fingers if the speaker is expressing surprise. Be sure to vary the order in which you say the two versions of each question.

---

[1] Do not correct errors involving the indirect object at this time. For example, a question such as "Who got for me a poster?" is acceptable.

Focused Practice (pages 180–182)

Exercise 1
autograph: a famous person's name, written by him or her

sign: to write your name

Exercise 2
license: an official piece of paper that allows you to own or do something

away: not at home or at work

Exercise 5
report: to tell someone in authority that something has happened

occur: to happen

ahead: in front of someone or something

insurance: money paid to a company that then agrees to pay an amount of money if something bad happens to you or your property

Communication Practice (pages 182–183)

Exercise 6
• You may need to define *damage* (harm that has been done to something).
• You may wish to have students read the script for this exercise in pairs. Monitor the questions for correct stress and intonation.

Exercise 7
• Students may not have seen questions with the structure *What* + noun + *did* + subject + verb as in "What sports did you play . . . ?" If necessary, model a few more questions like this, e.g., "What music did you like? / What TV shows did you watch? / What kind of music did you listen to . . . ?"
• To help students get started on this activity, brainstorm with the class. On the board write a list of topics they could ask each other about, e.g., school, sports, friends, pets, hobbies, their homes, teachers, traveling, accidents, marriage, jobs.

Exercise 8
Model the activity before students do it in pairs. Complete the sentences in the book and have the students take turns asking you questions with *who, what, when, where, why.*

Exercise 9
• Have students walk around and mingle as they do this activity.

• Follow up by saying names of students and having other students make sentences about them based on the information they recorded in their charts. For example:

T: Yolanda

S1: Her father taught her to ride a bike.

S2: Her grandmother read stories to her.

Further Practice
Before class, arrange for one student to pretend that he or she had a car accident. Work out the details with the student, e.g., how, where, and when the accident happened. Have the student pretend to limp, or tie up the student's arm in a "bandage." Have the student enter the classroom a few minutes late, after the other students are settled. When the student enters the room, pretend to be shocked and say, "What happened to you?" The student should answer, "I had an accident." Write *who, what, when, where, why, how* on the board. Instruct the class to ask *yes / no* and *wh-* questions to find out what happened. For example:
• When did the accident happen?
• Where did it happen?
• Why did you go there?
• Who was with you?
• Did the other driver stop?
• Did anyone help you?
• What happened to your car?

Conclude the questioning by saying, for example, "Well, Alex, we're sorry about your car, but we're happy that you're OK." Put students in pairs or small groups. Have them ask and answer questions about a real accident that they were or someone they know was involved in.

GRAMMAR OUT OF THE BOX . . . . . .

What's the news? Students will read and summarize a news story, and then they will answer a partner's questions about it. Make a handout like the following and give one to each student.

Title: _____

Who	What	When	Where	Why

Bring in short news stories. Give one to each student. Instruct students to read their stories and summarize the important information by filling in the chart. Put students in pairs. Instruct them to ask questions about their partner's story until they understand everything that happened. They must ask a minimum of five questions. They may not look at their partner's notes.

UNIT 24 Subject and Object Pronouns

Unit Overview

In Unit 24 students will learn about subject and object pronouns.

Grammar in Context (pages 187–188)

Comprehension Questions

- Who is an American? *(Kathy)*
- What does Carlos want to get? *(a gift for Bill)*
- What gift does Kathy suggest? *(chocolates)*
- Who is Bill? *(Carlos's boss)*
- What is Kathy's "price" for driving Carlos and Tomiko to the party? *(a box of chocolates)*
- Is Kathy serious? *(No, she's joking.)*

Words

- Have students look at the picture of *a ride.* Ask, "Who is giving a ride?" *(the driver)* "Who is getting a ride?" *(the couple)*
- Ask the students who has a car. Ask those who raise their hands if they often give rides to their friends.
- Write the idioms *give a ride* and *get a ride* on the board.

Expressions

For each expression, ask students to paraphrase the meaning and explain how the speaker feels. For example:

- *I suppose so:* I think so. *(The speaker isn't sure.)*
- *I don't think so:* Not sure. *(The speaker is doubtful.)*
- *Not appropriate:* Not suitable, not right. *(The speaker disapproves.)*
- *Good idea:* It's a good suggestion. *(The speaker approves.)*

Working Together

Extend Part B by having students talk about someone they know, such as another teacher, an absent classmate, a boyfriend / girlfriend, or family member. Remind them to use all the expressions when talking about the various gifts.

Grammar Presentation (page 189)

Identify the Grammar

Subject Pronouns
- *You're an American.*
- *He has a wife.*
- *I'm not sure.*

Object Pronouns
- *Let me think.*
- *Can I give them to her?*
- *He's always eating them at his desk.*

Grammar Charts

- Write the example sentences on the board. Do a quick transformation drill with all the singular and plural subject pronouns. Use one of the sentences as a model. Point to yourself and to students to indicate which pronouns to use. For example, point to the first sentence, then point to yourself. Students say, "I'm an American." Next point directly to a student. The class says, "You're an American." Point to a male student sitting a short distance away. The class says "He's an American," etc.
- If further practice is needed, repeat, but this time the sentences should be truthful. Students may form negative sentences, e.g., "I don't have a wife. / We aren't Americans."
- For sentences with object pronouns, have students first identify the subject and the object of the sentences on the board. (Note: In the sentence "Let me think," the unstated subject is *You.*)
- To reinforce the word order in sentences with object pronouns, write sentences on strips of overhead transparency and cut each strip into individual words. Lay out the words randomly and call up students to put them in the correct order. If you do not have an overhead projector, write the words on the board in random order and have students write the sentence correctly.

- Drill the object pronouns in the same manner as the subject pronouns above. Point to yourself and to the students to indicate which person and number you want students to say.

Grammar Notes

Note 1 *(Exercise 2)*
- Make up a list of sentences with noun subjects. Have students change the nouns to pronouns. For example:

  T: Tina likes flowers.

  Ss: She likes flowers.

- A more communicative version would be to make false statements about students and have the class correct you. For example:

  T: Tina loves chocolate.

  Ss: That's not true. She doesn't like chocolate (at all).

  T: Sergei drives a Toyota.

  Ss: No, he drives a motorcycle.

Note 2 *(Exercises 2–3)*
- Prepare a list of foods. Include both singular and plural items. Hand out the list, write it on the board, or project it as a transparency. Put students in pairs and have them ask and answer questions following the pattern below:

  Item: green beans

  S1: Do you like green beans?

  S2: Yes, I like them. / No, I don't like them.

  Item: milk

  S2: Do you like milk?

  S1: Yes, I like it. / No, I don't like it.

- To demonstrate pronouns as objects of prepositions, act out a restaurant scene. On the board, write the names of five dinner entrees, e.g. *roast chicken, steak, Chinese chicken salad, roast beef, veggie burger.* Choose one student to play the role of server and send that student out of the room. Choose five other students to be the diners. Have them sit in front of the class.

- Call in the server. Pretend that he or she got all the orders mixed up. The server should try to match the entrees with the diners. The diners should correct his or her confusion, as follows:

  SERVER: Is the roast chicken for you [looking at one of the diners]?

  DINER 1: No, it's not. It's for her [pointing to another diner].

SERVER: Oh, OK. How about the veggie burger? Is it for you?

DINER 2: No, it's not for me. It's for him.

Note 3
It is sufficient to read this note with the students. No practice is necessary.

Note 4
- Inform the students that, as with *both,* some Americans sometimes use *all* to indicate that *you* is plural, e.g., "Where are you all going tonight?"
- *Both* can be used in two ways: *you both* or *both of you.* It is also correct to say *the two (three, etc.) of you.*

Focused Practice (pages 190–191)

Exercise 2
present: gift

plenty: a lot; a large amount

Exercise 3
a vest: a piece of clothing with no sleeves that you wear over a shirt

Communication Practice (page 192)

Exercise 5
- Before listening, check that students know these colors. Say each color and have the class point to a matching object, such as a piece of clothing.
- Ask the students what *something special* can be. (Possible answers: *something expensive, unusual, or hard to find*)
- Have students try to predict which gift will be for which person. Elicit, for example: "I think the tennis racquet is for Jeremy."

Exercise 6
Remind students to use the expressions on page 188.

Further Practice
In North America, many people observe the custom of spring cleaning. In early spring they clean their houses from top to bottom. They also go through their possessions and choose things they want to throw away, donate to charity, or give to people they know. Make three lists of items that the students "found"

while spring cleaning and decided to discard, or have students make their own lists. For example:

Student 1	Student 2	Student 3
a broken tennis racquet a new sweater that you never wore a set of yellow bath towels	uncomfortable shoes (size 8) in good condition a framed poster of Yosemite an electric coffee maker	an old bottle of juice a soccer ball a men's ski jacket, size Large

In class, explain the custom of spring cleaning to the class. (Most cultures have a similar custom.) Write a few items on the board and model the activity by saying, e.g., "I really don't need these things. I never use them. What should I do with them? Let's see . . . I can give the ski jacket to my brother. He likes to ski. What should I do with this sweater? I don't need it. What do you think?" Elicit suggestions from the class. Put students in groups of three. Instruct students to read their lists of items to their classmates. Their classmates should offer suggestions for what to do with the unwanted items. Encourage them to use their imaginations. For example:

- I wear size 8 shoes, so you can give them to me.
- Throw the tennis racquet away.
- Donate the ski jacket to the Red Cross.
- Paint your bathroom yellow and use the towels.

 **GRAMMAR OUT OF THE BOX ......**

Birthday present. Students will select a birthday present for a person everyone knows (e.g., you, another teacher, a student who is absent). Bring in a variety of catalogues: clothing, cars, gardening supplies, furniture, housewares. Try to have one catalogue for every four students. Explain the task. Students must work together to select a gift for the person you name. Give them a time limit. Instruct students to use Exercise 6 as a model for their conversation. When time is up, have each group tell the class which gift they selected for the person and why.

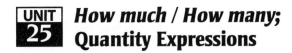 **UNIT 25** *How much / How many; Quantity Expressions*

Unit Overview

In Unit 25 students will learn the use of *how much* and *how many* to ask about quantities and the use of quantity expressions in answering questions.

Grammar in Context (pages 193–194)

Comprehension Questions
- Where did Jessica and Tim go? *(Ecuador)*
- How many days were they away? *(10)*
- Which places did they visit? *(the capital, Quito, and the Galápagos Islands)*
- Where did they sleep? *(on a boat)*
- Was the trip expensive? *(yes)*

Words
- Ask students for the names of other islands they know.
- Ask them to name the capital of their country or province.

Expressions
- Ask several students: "Where did you go on your last vacation? How long were you away?"
- Ask the class to explain *I'll bet. (It means Speaker B believes what Speaker A said.)* Contrast it with *You said it* (which means Speaker B strongly agrees with Speaker A). Give additional examples of each expression, e.g.:

  —A: I was sad when my dog died.

  B: I'll bet.

  —A: This weather is too cold for me.

  B: You said it.

- *Don't ask* in this case implies that the trip was very expensive. In general it is a substitute for a negative or unpleasant reply, e.g.:

  A: How was the meeting?

  B: Don't ask. *(The meeting was bad.)*

Working Together
- If possible, have students talk about a place they visited in the city where your school is located. (Students will talk about their vacations in a later activity.)

- Model answers to the questions by talking about a museum, park, etc., you visited.

Grammar Presentation (page 195)

Identify the Grammar

- *How many days were you away?*
- *How much time did you spend there?*
- *How many people were on the boat?*
- *How much did the trip cost?*

Grammar Charts

Ask the following questions to help students identify the use of *how many* and *how much*:
- What kind of noun comes after *how many*? *(plural count)*
- Which words and expressions can we use to answer a question with *how many*? *(a lot, not many, a few, or a number)*
- What kind of noun comes after *how much*? *(non-count)*
- Which words and expressions can we use to answer a question with *how much*? *(a lot, not much, a little, a number + a noun)*
- Is it necessary to put a noun after *how much* or *how many*? *(no)*

Grammar Notes

Note 1   *(Exercises 2–3)*
- Compile a list of count and non-count nouns the students have learned. Conduct a drill in which you say a noun and the students respond with *how much* or *how many*. For example:

    —T: flowers

    Ss: how many flowers

    —T: roast beef

    Ss: how much roast beef

- Alternatively, have students write a list of six to eight foods they ate in the past two days. Put them in pairs. They should ask each other about the quantity of each food the other student ate, for example, *milk, potato chips*:

    —S1: How much milk did you drink?

    S2: Two glasses.

    —S1: How many potato chips did you eat?

    S2: About 200!

Note 2
- Write the following words on the board in random order: *a lot, a few, some, a little, not much, not many.* Instruct students to put

them in order from the largest to the smallest quantity using a chart like the following: (Note: The correct answers are provided here.)

Count	Non-count
a lot	a lot
some	some
a few	a little
not many	not much

- Have students practice asking questions and giving answers. Write a mix of plural count and non-count nouns on the board, e.g.; *free time, money, friends, CDs, pairs of shoes,* etc. Put students in pairs and tell them to take turns asking questions with *how much* + non-count noun and *how many* + count noun. Partners should answer truthfully using the quantifiers in the chart.

Note 3   *(Exercises 2–3)*
Have students do a lineup. Students ask each other a question with *how many*, answer with a number, and line up from the smallest to the largest number. It is best to choose a question that can have a wide range of answers. For example:
- How many cousins do you have?
- How many pairs of shoes do you own?
- How many books did you read last year?

Note 4   *(Exercises 2–3)*
- Cut out pictures of various consumer items from magazines or catalogues. There should be a picture for every student in the class.
- Hand out the pictures. Instruct students to pretend they own the item in their picture and to imagine what it cost.
- Put students in pairs and have them ask and answer questions about the cost of "their" items. Encourage them to explain their answers. For example:

A: How much was your watch?

B: $125. How much did your shoes cost?

A: Only $25. I got them on sale.

→ For additional practice, see the Supplementary Activities on page 91.

Focused Practice (pages 196–198)

Exercise 2
Capitol: the building in Washington, D.C., where the U.S. Congress meets

round trip: a trip from one place to another and back again

share: to have or use something together with other people

Exercise 3
provide: to give something to someone

Communication Practice (pages 198–199)

Exercise 5
• The blanks before the text are for Part A. The blanks following the text are for Part B.
• Have students read the items before listening. Ask them to tell what they know about John Phillips without listening. For example, they can infer that he was a travel writer, he had children and grandchildren, and he left his money to a number of people.

Exercise 6
Partners can use either *how much* or *how many* to ask for the exact amount. For example, they can ask, "How much did you drink? / How many cups of coffee did you drink?"

Exercise 7
You may want to have students use the items in the box for Part A. For Part B they can write their own questions and record the answers in the chart.

Further Practice
Have students sit in groups of three and take turns asking and answering questions about their best vacation. They can use the conversation on page 193 as a model. If possible they should bring photos of the trip; if they do not have any, perhaps they can print out a map or images of the place from the Internet.

GRAMMAR OUT OF THE BOX . . . . . .

Healthy lifestyles. In this activity students will interview each other about their lifestyles. Students can work with one partner or in small groups. Make copies of the survey below, or make up another one similar to it. Have students interview one another by asking questions beginning with *How much / many* _____ *do you get / have/ eat / etc.?* For

example, "How much stress do you have in your life?" After the interviews, have two pairs or two small groups sit together. Each student should report on one other student's lifestyle. For example:
• Paulina sleeps a lot, more than eight hours each night.
• She drinks a little tea, maybe two or three cups a week.
• She exercises almost every day.
• I think her lifestyle is pretty healthy.

How much / many	a lot	some	a few / a little / not much / not many	none
sleep				
exercise				
stress				
caffeine				
cigarettes				
sugar				
fat				
fruits and vegetables				
close friends				

UNIT 26 *There is / There are*

Unit Overview

In Unit 26 students will learn the use of *There is / There are* in statements and questions.

Grammar in Context (pages 200–201)

Comprehension Questions
• Where are Amanda and Josh? *(in London, at Victoria Station)*
• What do they need? *(a place to stay)*
• Where do they go for help? *(an information booth)*
• Where are Amanda and Josh going to stay? *(at a bed-and-breakfast)*

Words
• Ask the class who took a vacation recently. Ask those students who did where they stayed, and use the context to explain *youth hostel* and *bed-and-breakfast.* If students don't understand the difference, explain that a youth hostel is like an inexpensive hotel for students and young people. Usually there are

many people in one room and the shower is down the hall. A bed-and-breakfast is usually a room in someone's house. It can be cheap or expensive, but it always includes breakfast.

- If your city does not have an Underground (subway) and students don't know what it is, give examples of cities that have subways, e.g., London, New York, Tokyo.

- Ask students to look at the picture and tell what they know about *snack bars*. For example, they serve fast food such as sandwiches; you eat at a counter, not a table; they are found most often at train or bus stations and airports.

Expressions

Call on pairs of students to read the dialogues in front of the class, and then elicit paraphrases or explanations of the new expressions:

- *lead the way* = take me there
- Explain that *would you like* is a very polite way of offering to do something for someone. *Please do* is a formal reply.
- *hold* = keep
- *My pleasure* is similar to *You're welcome*. It is formal. *Enjoy your stay* is often used by people in the travel industry at the end of a conversation with clients or guests.

Working Together

Follow up Part B by asking students if there are any other special attractions in their town / city / neighborhood. You could also ask them to recommend three places that visitors to their town should visit.

Grammar Presentation (pages 202–203)

Identify the Grammar

- *There's* an information booth over there.
- *Are there* any youth hostels around here?
- *There are* a few inexpensive ones.
- *Is there* anything else I can help you with?

Grammar Charts

Ask questions like the following to help students understand the structure and use of *there is / there are*:

- What kind of noun comes after *there is*? (*singular count or non-count*)
- What is the negative form of *there is*? (*there isn't*)

- What kind of noun comes after *there are*? (*plural*)
- How do we form the negative? (*there aren't*)
- What is the word order in *yes / no* questions? (*Is / are + there + noun*)
- How do we form affirmative short answers? (*Yes, there is / there are*)
- How do we form negative short answers? (*No, there isn't / there aren't*)

Grammar Notes

Note 1 *(Exercise 2)* and **Note 5**
Inform students that one common use of *there is / are* is to describe what is in a location such as a room.

- To practice, have students form sentences about your classroom, e.g., "There's a bulletin board next to the door. / There are six windows."
- Alternatively, make copies of a picture that shows a lot of people and actions. Put students in pairs and distribute one picture, facedown, to each pair. At your signal, instruct students to turn over the photo and look at it for a very short time (15–30 seconds). Then have them turn the picture over again.
- In pairs, students should form sentences with *there is / are* based on what they can remember. The pair that makes the most true sentences "wins."

Note 2
In Working Together students spoke about attractions in their towns. Extend by having them write down desirable things that are *not* found in their town. Go around the room and have each student form a sentence such as:

- In _____ there are a lot of parks, but there isn't an art museum.
- There isn't a McDonald's in my town.

Notes 3 and 4 *(Exercises 2–3)*
Put students in pairs to practice asking and answering questions. Have them ask each other about the contents of their backpacks or purses. For example:

S1: Is there a cell phone in your backpack?

S2: Yes, there is. How about you?

S1: No, there isn't. I don't have a cell phone.

S2: Oh, OK. Well, are there any pencils in your backpack?

S1: Yes, there are.

Note 6 *(Exercises 2, 4)*

• Choose a room in your home and have the class ask you questions about it using *is there / are there*. Answer using *it* or *they*. For example:

S: Is there a television in your living room?

T: Yes, it's in the corner.

• Put students in pairs or small groups and have them do the same. They can talk about a room in their parents' home or the place where they are now living.

Focused Practice (pages 203–205)

Exercise 1
biscuits: (British) cookies

Exercise 3
inch: 2.54 centimeters

Exercise 4
scene: the place where something happens
Stay tuned: Continue listening.

Exercise 5
sign off: to say good-bye at the end of a letter

Communication Practice (page 206)

Exercise 6
• Before listening, ask students if they know where Manchester is. If you have a map, show them where it is compared to London.
• Have students read the questions and see if they can answer them before listening. For example, students may know that the American word for *Underground* is *subway* or *metro*. (By the way, for fun you can ask students what the British call their Underground. The answer is *the tube*.)

Exercise 7
Before beginning the game, have each student compose a sentence to use in the game. Tell students to make sure their sentence includes an adjective + noun combination (e.g., *cheap DVD player, two blue soccer balls*).

Further Practice
This is an activity that sounds silly but in fact generates a great deal of laughter and discussion because it reveals a great deal about students' preferences and lifestyles. Have students make a list of the contents of their refrigerator. Remind them to use count and

non-count nouns and quantifiers (see Unit 25). Have them sit in small groups and share information using *there is* and *there are*. Encourage students to form negative sentences as well, e.g.:

S1: There are three bottles of milk in my refrigerator.

S2: There isn't any milk in my refrigerator.

S1: Why not?

S2: I don't like milk.

Picture differences. Create two versions of a simple drawing of a room. Include different details in each room, e.g., one picture has a vase of flowers on the table, the other doesn't. Have students work in pairs. Explain the task: They need to ask each other *yes / no* questions with *Is there . . . ? Are there . . . ?* in order to find the differences between the two pictures. For example:

S1: Is there a picture of a dog next to the telephone?

S2: No, there isn't. There's a picture of a cat.

S1: Are there three windows in your picture?

S2: Yes, there are.

Tell students in advance how many differences there are between the two pictures.

UNIT 27 Noun and Adjective Modifiers

Unit Overview

In Unit 27 students will learn how to use adjectives and nouns to modify other nouns in phrases such as *a young computer scientist*.

Grammar in Context (pages 210–211)

Comprehension Questions
Which man or woman . . .
• is a chemistry teacher? *(man C)*
• enjoys fast cars? *(woman B)*
• likes jazz bands? *(man A)*
• is young and artistic? *(woman A)*
• is rich? *(man B and woman C)*

Words

- Pantomime the adjectives *athletic, romantic, young-at-heart,* and *easygoing,* and try to elicit descriptions from the students for, e.g., *good at sports*.
- Ask the students to name people who match each description, e.g., "Who is an athletic man? / Who has a young-at-heart grandfather?"
- For the noun + noun combinations, ask questions such as:
  —What is a famous spy movie? *(any James Bond film)*
  —What was the name of your high school chemistry teacher?
  —Is anyone in the class a computer science major?

Expressions

- Ask a few more students what subjects they are interested in. You can also do this in a chain, with Student A asking Student B, Student B asking Student C, and so forth.
- Have students paraphrase *get together (meet)*.

Working Together

For Part B, extend by asking the students if any of the people in the ads are possible matches for *them*. Why or why not?

Grammar Presentation (pages 212–213)

Identify the Grammar

- *I'm* <u>easygoing</u>.
- *a* <u>kind, sensitive</u> *woman*
- *Enjoys* <u>spy</u> *films and* <u>abstract</u> *art*.
- <u>Tall, slim, 25-year-old chemistry</u> *teacher*.

Grammar Charts

- Write the example sentences on the board.
- Ask questions to help students identify the various ways the nouns and adjectives can combine. Point to the underlined words in the items on the board and ask students if each word is an adjective or a noun. As they respond, write "formulas" on the board to describe the combinations, e.g.:
  —*be + adjective*
  —*adjective + noun*
  —*noun + noun*
  —*adjective + adjective + noun*

- Have students match the formulas with the different charts. For each chart, elicit a few similar phrases from the students.

Grammar Notes

Note 1 *(Exercises 2–3)*
- To reinforce the information, write a noun on the board, e.g., *music*. Quickly point to students around the room and ask them to say different adjective + noun phrases. (*soft music, loud music, rap music,* etc.)
- Be prepared to explain that in noun + noun combinations, the first noun acts as an adjective.

Note 2 *(Exercises 2–3)*
Do a transformation drill as follows:
T: [choose an adjective] smart
S1: He is smart.
S2: He's a smart student.

Note 3 *(Exercises 2–3)*
- Inevitably a student will ask you about the difference between *interesting / interested, bored / boring,* etc. To explain, provide a pair of sentences like the following:
  The movie was interesting.
  I was interested in the movie.
- Ask students questions to clarify: What was interesting? Who was interested?
- Provide other examples, e.g.:
  —The lesson was boring / I was bored.
  —John was excited about the trip to Disneyland / The trip was exciting.

Note 4 *(Exercises 2–3)*
For multi-word adjectives, explain that the hyphen connects all the words and makes them function as one.

Note 6 *(Exercises 2-3)*
- Make a game out of trying to find adjectives that start with vowels. Divide the class into small groups and assign each group a vowel. The group's task is to think of adjectives beginning with that letter. For example:
  a—amazing, artistic; e—elegant, energetic; i—interesting, individual; o—open, ordinary; u—ugly, unusual
- After the groups have made their lists, call on each student to say a phrase consisting of *an* + adjective + noun, e.g., *an open door*. Have the class repeat each phrase.

Note 7 *(Exercises 2–3)*

- Play a pyramid game to reinforce the grammar point. Draw a pyramid on the board or on a handout. Divide it into five horizontal sections. In the top triangle of the pyramid, write an adjective + noun combination, e.g., *a smart girl*.
- Put students in groups of two or three. Each student expands the phrase by adding an adjective and writing the new phrase in the next section of the pyramid.
- Have each group share its longest sentence with the whole class.

Focused Practice (pages 213–215)

Exercise 1

band: a group of people who play music together

interest: something you do or study because you enjoy it

Exercise 2

dress: (verb) to put clothes on someone or on yourself

baggy: baggy clothes fit very loosely

brick: a hard block of baked clay, used for building

Exercise 3

date: an arrangement to meet a boyfriend or girlfriend

Exercise 4

cable TV: a system of television that is paid for by the person who owns the TV

Communication Practice (pages 215–217)

Exercise 5

Before listening, have students use the language they know to describe each of the people in the picture. To save time you may wish to create seven small groups and assign one person to each group, which then shares its description with the class.

Exercise 6

- After finishing Part A, check to make sure students understand the new words *generous, stingy, mean.* Perhaps they can name a character from literature, history, movies, or a television program that fits each of these adjectives.
- For Part B, model by making sentences about well-known people, e.g., "George Washington was an honest president."

Exercise 7

- If possible bring in samples of the materials in the box. Hold up each sample and say the word, or display samples on your desk, say each name, and have a student select the matching material.
- Elicit other materials from the students and write them on the board.

Exercise 8

A fun twist on this activity is to have students guess who wrote each letter. They can write their guesses on the bottom of each letter posted on the wall and see how many of them guessed the right person.

Further Practice

Put students in small groups and have them re-read the letter to Dahlia on page 215. Instruct them to make a list of all the possible solutions to Rosa's problem. For example:

- Rosa should break up with Joe and find a more generous man.
- Rosa should pay for their dates.
- Rosa should have one of Joe's friends talk to him.
- She should talk to Joe and tell him how she feels.

Next, students should look at their list, discuss each suggestion, and in the end choose the one they think is best. Have one student from each group share that group's solution.

It is also possible to have students write their responses like newspaper advice columnists. The responses can be posted on the wall, or students can sit in groups and read their responses to their classmates.

 GRAMMAR OUT OF THE BOX ......

What's important in love? Have students sit in pairs or small groups and discuss the question "What is important to you in love?" Consider these topics:

- Age (e.g., young, middle-aged, old)
- Looks (e.g., tall, dark, beautiful / handsome)
- Personality (e.g., kind, friendly, romantic)
- Profession (e.g., an athlete, an engineer, a teacher)
- Likes and dislikes (e.g., romantic music, mysteries, tennis)

Examples:

- I want someone close to my age.

- I like black hair and blue eyes.
- I prefer a quiet woman.

Which item is the *most* important to you? Second? Third?

UNIT 28 Comparative Adjectives

Unit Overview

In Unit 28 students will learn regular and irregular comparative adjectives.

Grammar in Context (pages 218–219)

Comprehension Questions

- When is the party? *(Saturday night at about 8:00)*
- How many people are coming? *(15)*
- What kind of music is good for dancing? *(rock)*
- What food do they decide to have? *(pizza)*
- What kind of entertainment do they choose? *(games)*

Words

- Ask students to look at the illustration and tell you what kind of list this is *(a shopping list)*. Give, or ask students for, other types of lists. For example, you could write a "to do" list on the board.
- Ask students to tell what type of entertainment they see in the drawing *(CDs and video games)*. Elicit other types of entertainment, such as reading, watching TV, dancing, etc. Then ask the students to define the term *entertainment (things we do for fun)*.
- Elicit names of games and list them on the board. Ask students for the name of their favorite game.

Expressions

- In all three conversations, Speaker A makes a suggestion and Speaker B responds. Ask the class:
  —What are two ways of making a suggestion? *(What about . . . and How about . . .)*
  —How do we respond if we like a suggestion? *(Sounds good.)*
  —What can we say if we don't like a suggestion? *(I'm tired of . . .)*

- Elicit other things we can say if we don't like a suggestion and write them on the board. For example:
  —*No thanks.*
  —*I don't think so.*
  —*That's not a good idea.*

Working Together

If students are at a loss, give them pairs of movies that have something in common, such as two films in the same series, a modern remake of an old film, two movies with the same actor, two films with the same theme, etc.

Grammar Presentation (pages 220–221)

Identify the Grammar

- *It's a lot <u>better</u> for dancing.*
- *It's <u>easier</u> and <u>quicker than</u> steak.*
- *Who's <u>faster</u>? Who's <u>smarter</u>? Who's <u>funnier</u>?*
- *Games are <u>more interesting</u> than videos.*

Grammar Charts

Write the examples from the reading on the board. Have students look at the charts and the examples on the board and answer the following questions:
- If an adjective has one syllable, how do we form the comparative? *(add -er)*
- If an adjective ends in *-y*, how do we form the comparative? *(change the -y to -i and add -er)*
- If an adjective is longer than one syllable, how do we form the comparative? *(more + adjective)*
- Which word often comes after the adjective? *(than)*

Grammar Notes

Notes 1 and 2   *(Exercises 2–3)*
- Write a set of one-syllable adjectives on the board, e.g.: *fast, slow, tall, short, quick, young, old*
- Using facts about students in the class, model several sentences with comparative adjectives. For example: "Sonia is taller than Hannah. She's also younger."
- Name other pairs of students and elicit sentences from the class.

Note 3 *(Exercises 2–3)*
- Provide a list of adjectives like the following one: *funny, easy, dirty, pretty, sunny, rainy, messy, happy, busy, friendly*
- Call on students to use comparative adjectives to compose sentences about people, places, or things, e.g.: "Chris Rock is funnier than Jackie Chan."
- Invite a second student to disagree with the first, e.g.: "I disagree. I think Jackie Chan is funnier."

Note 4 *(Exercises 2–3)*
Repeat the procedure from Note 3 using the following list of adjectives: *interesting, beautiful, difficult, expensive, crowded, dangerous, famous, serious, intelligent*. For example:

S1: Tokyo is more expensive than Houston.

S2: It's also more crowded.

Notes 5 and 6 *(Exercises 2–3)*
Put students in pairs. Make two lists of items like the ones below, and give a different list to each student. Have students ask and answer questions using *better* or *worse*, e.g.:

S1: Which is better, steak or chicken?

S2: I think steak is better.

S2: Which is worse, a headache or a stomachache?

S1: For me a headache is worse.

S1	S2
Friday night, Saturday night	headache, stomachache
rain, snow	the beach, the mountains
washing dishes, drying dishes	waking up early, going to bed late
steak, chicken	bad music, a bad movie
dancing, singing	flowers, chocolate

Focused Practice *(pages 221–223)*

Exercise 1
level: a standard of skill or ability in a particular subject

original: first, earliest

remake: a record or movie that has the same music or story as one that was made before

Exercise 4
tricks: a set of actions done to entertain people

protective: wanting to protect someone from danger or harm

bark: when a dog barks, it makes a short loud sound

rule: (informal) used in order to say that the team, school, place, person, etc., mentioned is better than any other.

Communication Practice *(page 224)*

Exercise 5
Have students read the questions and make inferences about Ken before listening. Ask them: *What do we know about Ken?* For example, they can infer that Ken is a student, that he has a grandmother.

Exercise 6
- If possible, make use of the list of games you wrote on the board for the Words activity.
- If it is not possible to talk about games, students can talk about sports such as ice skating / roller skating, soccer / football, baseball / rugby, skiing / snowboarding, etc.

Exercise 7
- Students will work in groups of three to select the items for each topic.
- Then students will divide the *first three* topics in the chart among the three group members. That is, each student will compare item 1 and item 2 for one topic.
- Each student will then survey the group members, including himself or herself, on his or her topic.
- Students will then express opinions one-by-one on the final topic, and all will enter the results in their charts.
- If the class is small, the group can report its results to the whole class. If the class is large, put two groups together and have them report the results to one another.

Further Practice
Make a comparison circle.[1] Prepare sets of eight related items and write them in a circle on a handout or overhead transparency, like this:

orange juice

water   lemonade

Coca-Cola   milk

tea   coffee

hot chocolate

Students can work as a whole class or in groups of four. To determine which student goes first, use a die or have students draw

---

[1] Based on the Activity Circle comparisons in Penny Ur, *Grammar Practice Activities* (Cambridge: Cambridge University Press, 1988).

numbers out of a hat. The first student to have a turn should draw a line from one item to another and make a comparison using known adjectives (including *good* and *bad*), e.g., "Hot chocolate is tastier than milk." Students may not repeat an adjective that has already been used. In case students have difficulty, you may wish to prepare an "adjective bank" ahead of time. Other sets of nouns that will work nicely in this game can be drawn from animals, clothing items, jobs, cities, vacation destinations, methods of transportation, famous people such as singers or actors, types of entertainment.

 OUT OF THE BOX . . . . . .

Class party. Using the opening conversation on page 218 as a model, have students plan a real or imaginary class party. Have each student join one of the following "committees": food, drink, decorations, entertainment. Each committee should make a list of possible choices. Then the group members should compare the choices and decide on the best one or ones. As an example, a list of possible decorations could include: balloons, flowers, streamers, colored lights. Each committee should report to the whole class what it decided.

UNIT
29 **Superlative Adjectives**

Unit Overview

In Unit 29 students will learn the regular and irregular superlative forms of adjectives.

Grammar in Context (pages 225–226)

Comprehension Questions

- Where did Amanda and Josh go? *(England / Great Britain)*
- What was the most exciting place they visited? *(London)*
- What was the most interesting place? *(Stonehenge)*
- How was the weather? *(hot)*
- What dangerous thing happened? *(Josh drove in the wrong direction.)*

Words

Have students look at the pictures and use them to explain *pouring rain, soaked, flat tire, honking.*

Expressions

- By now students will certainly understand *I agree.* Depending on your students' first languages, you may need to point out that *agree* is a verb in English. (In many languages it is an adjective.) Therefore, it is wrong to say *I am agree.*
- Have students explain what *turned out OK* and *Tell you what* mean:
  —*turned out OK:* In the end, nothing bad happened.
  —*Tell you what:* This expression is used for introducing a suggestion.

Working Together

Model Part B by telling about your best or most interesting trip.

Grammar Presentation (pages 227–228)

Identify the Grammar
- *What was <u>the best</u> thing about your trip?*
- *That was <u>the most exciting</u> place.*
- *It was also <u>the worst</u> part of the trip.*
- *This is <u>the hottest</u> summer in Europe in 10 years.*
- *It was <u>the most terrible</u> night I can remember.*
- *<u>The</u> two <u>scariest</u> things happened when we were driving.*

Grammar Charts

Write the examples from the opening reading on the board. Have students look at the charts and the examples on the board and answer the following questions:
- Which word is part of every superlative? *(the)*
- If an adjective has one syllable, how do we form the superlative? *(add -est to the adjective)*
- If an adjective ends in *-y*, how do we form the superlative? *(change the y to i and add -est to the adjective)*
- If an adjective is longer than one syllable, how do we form the superlative? *(the most + adjective)*

- *The best* is the superlative of which adjective? *(good)*
- *The worst* is the superlative of which adjective? *(bad)*

Grammar Notes

Notes 1–2 *(Exercise 2)*
- Write a set of one-word adjectives on the board, e.g.: *fast, slow, tall, short, smart, quick, young, old, rich, poor, large, small.*
- Model the superlative of one-syllable adjectives by talking about animals. An unusual approach would be to bring in pictures of different dog breeds or birds. Then you could make sentences like the following:
  —The German shepherd is the largest. It is also the smartest.
  —The chihuahua is the smallest.
- Show several more sets of pictures and have the students form similar sentences.

Note 3 *(Exercise 2)*
- Bring in several magazine pictures of people. If possible, use close-ups so that students can focus on the faces.
- Provide a list of adjectives than end in *-y*, e.g.: *funny, pretty, happy, busy, friendly, lucky, messy*
- Show the pictures in sets of three. Ask questions using the superlative form of the adjectives in the box. Have students give their opinions. Invite other students to disagree. For example:
  T: [holds up three pictures] Which person is the friendliest?
  S1: I think the girl in the middle is the friendliest.
  S2: I think the man is the friendliest. He's smiling.

Note 4 *(Exercise 2)*
- Repeat the procedure used in Notes 2 and 3. Put a list of longer words on the board. For example: *interesting, beautiful, difficult, expensive, crowded, dangerous, famous, serious, intelligent*
- Model sentences using the superlative. Invite students to respond. For example, "I think sky-diving is the most dangerous sport. What do you think?"
- Have each student write a similar sentence using an adjective from the list. Put students in pairs to share, or go around the room in a chain.

Note 5
Write a list of popular foods on the board. Then have students say which restaurant serves the best and worst versions of each dish. Invite them to disagree with each other. For example:
Item: fish tacos
S1: I think Pescado Fresh has the best fish tacos.
S2: No way! They use too much oil. The best fish tacos are at (restaurant).

Note 6
- Call on students to answer a variety of questions about their experiences. For example:
  T: What was your happiest day?
  S: My happiest day was the day my daughter was born.
- After doing a few questions with the whole class, have students continue asking and answering questions in pairs. If necessary, write a few more adjectives on the board, e.g., *sad, funny, strange, scary.*

Focused Practice (pages 228–230)

Exercise 1
you guys: (spoken) you people, used for both men and women

collection: a set of similar things which have been brought together

open-air: outdoor

amazing: very surprising and exciting

Exercise 2
country: the land that is outside a city or town

spare: a spare (tire) is an extra one that you keep or have in case you need it

Exercise 3
ridiculous: very silly

Communication Practice (pages 230–231)

Exercise 4
- After listening, find out if any of the students in the class collect stamps. Ask them to talk about their collection, using the adjectives in the box.
- If no one collects stamps, ask about other collections, such as coins, comic books, etc.

Exercise 5

Invite students to talk about other sports which may not be in the box, such as snowboarding, sky-diving, volleyball, gymnastics, etc.

Exercise 6

For Part C, have each group choose one person to tell the class about that group's discussion. Instruct the speaker to tell the class three things that the group agreed on, e.g.: "We agree that the most beautiful city is Paris. The most important holiday is Independence Day. And the funniest actor is Jim Carrey."

Further Practice

In this activity, students will choose a unique superlative to describe each of their classmates, similar to a senior-class Hall of Fame in U.S. high schools. Before class, create an even number of small groups. Write the names of the group members on a card. In class, put students in their groups and distribute the cards. Explain the task and give examples. In high schools, it's common for students to vote for the boy and girl who are Most Athletic, Most Popular, Best Looking, etc. In your class, every student will receive a unique superlative designation. Encourage students to pick affectionate, positive superlatives for the people on their card. Funny superlatives—"Sleepiest Student" for a student who always takes a short nap during the break, or "Thirstiest" for a student who is constantly drinking—work well. At the end, go around the room and have each group say the superlatives it picked for each student. If there is time, you can have students create a crown, banner, or "certificate" with each student's superlative on it.

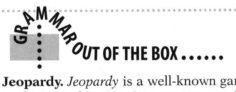
GRAMMAR OUT OF THE BOX ......

Jeopardy. *Jeopardy* is a well-known game show in the United States. Contestants are given the answers to questions in a category of their choice. They provide the questions. For example, in the category of geography, a contestant would read: *the lowest place in the world.* The correct answer would be, "Where / What is the Dead Sea?"

Preparation
• Prepare a Jeopardy game to play with the class. For categories and questions, a good source is the *Guinness Book of World Records.* (There is also a website.) The number of

categories and questions you prepare will depend on the size of your class; four or five categories with five questions in each are usually enough. Categories that work well include animals, cities, geography, weather, people, art, languages, sports, and anything else that your students are interested in.
• Decide in advance how you will score the game. One option is simply to give one point for each correct question. (Remember: You provide the answers. Contestants provide the questions.) You may also wish to include "bonus" answers worth two points each.
• Write each answer on one side of an index card. Write the questions on the other side. Organize the questions into categories.

Procedure
• Write the categories on the board. Lay the groups of index cards on a desk or table.
• Divide the class into two teams. Two students at a time will play the game.
• Toss a coin to decide which team goes first.
• The person whose turn it is chooses a category. The "host" then reads an answer. The student responds with a question. If the question is correct, the team scores a point. If the question is incorrect, the other team gets a chance to form the correct question.
• A student who has had a turn goes to the end of the line.
• The game ends when all the answers have been used or when time is up.

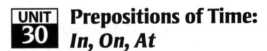
UNIT 30 Prepositions of Time: *In, On, At*

Unit Overview

In Unit 30 students will learn the use of *in*, *on*, and *at* in time expressions.

Grammar in Context (pages 232–233)

Comprehension Questions
• Where and when did Tim and Felix meet? (*on the train to Seattle in August*)
• Why is Felix calling? (*to invite Tim and his wife to a barbecue*)
• When is it? (*on Saturday the 20th at 2:30 in the afternoon*)

Words

- Ask the students if they've even been to a barbecue. Then ask follow-up questions about the place, time, type of food, guests, etc.
- If no one has been to a barbecue, explain what it is (a meal that is cooked and eaten outside).
- Have students look at the picture of the two-story house. Explain that a two-*story* house has two levels or two floors. Ask if any of the students live in a two-story house.

Expressions

None of these expressions can be understood literally, so you may need to explain them to the students as follows:

- *call you back:* This expression means to return someone's phone call, that is, to telephone someone after he or she has called you.
- *We're free:* The speaker has no other plans and can accept an invitation.
- *Just yourselves:* When someone is invited to dinner in the United States, it is common to offer to bring something to eat or drink. If the host does not want the guest to bring anything, he or she may respond this way.
- *looking forward to it:* The speaker is excited about an event in the future.

Working Together
Part B

Divide the class into five groups and assign one announcement to each group. Have them work together to say what the event in their announcement is. Then call on one student from each group to report on the group's sentence. Correct errors as needed.

Grammar Presentation (page 234)

> ### Identify the Grammar
> - *We met in August.*
> - *On Saturday, the 20th, in the afternoon.*
> - *We're free on the 20th.*
> - *Come at about 2:30.*

Grammar Charts

- Write the examples from the opening reading on the board. Read through each column on the chart and point to the examples on the board that use each preposition.

- Call on students to provide additional examples like the ones in the charts. For example, the chart has *in 2007*. Encourage students to say *in 1975, in 2000,* etc.
- Correct any errors that arise.

Grammar Notes

Note 1   *(Exercises 2–3)*
- On the board, write a year, a month, one or two parts of the day. The times you select should be meaningful to you in some way.
- Instruct students to ask you questions with *in* and the times you wrote on the board. For example: "What happened in 1973? / Is your birthday in August? / Do you like to sleep in the afternoon?"
- Answer the students' questions in complete sentences.

Note 2   *(Exercises 2–3)*
Repeat the procedure from Note 1.

Note 3   *(Exercises 2–3)*
Repeat the procedure from Note 1.

→ For additional practice, see the Supplementary Activities on page 92.

Focused Practice (pages 234–236)

Exercise 1
reach: to speak to someone who is not with you, especially by telephone

Communication Practice (pages 237–238)

Exercise 5
Before listening, have students read the information in each column so that they know what to listen for. Have them predict whether they'll need to use *on* or *at* in each column.

Exercise 6
One way to have all your students share what they learned is to go around the room and have each student tell one surprising thing they learned about one of their classmates.

Exercise 7
Instruct students to write down the answers their partners give them. Follow up the activity by having students say or write complete sentences about the information they heard. For example, "Americans vote on a Tuesday. / The French vote on a Sunday."

Exercise 8

- Instruct students not to show anyone the sentence they write.
- When they tell the class about their event, they should say only the first part of the sentence they wrote, e.g.:
  —My sister got married . . .
  —I graduated from college . . .

Further Practice

Students will find out some important events that occurred on their birthday or another day they choose. Instruct students to do an Internet search for "this date in history." There are quite a few sites of this kind. Tell them to choose one, then select the date they want to read about. Have them record at least three events that occurred on the date they chose. For example, they could write down someone who was born on that day, someone who died, and another important event. Put students in groups and have them report on what they found. They can begin as follows: "Several important things happened on January 18. First, I was born at 11:20 A.M. in 1982. Also, . . ."

 GRAMMAR OUT OF THE BOX . . . . . .

Conversation about holidays. In this activity students will talk about their favorite holiday. Put students in groups of four. If possible, put students from different countries together. Instruct students to pick one holiday and provide details about the way people in their country, town, or family celebrate it. They can include the following information:
- When the holiday is celebrated
- What happens at different times of the day
- What clothes people wear
- What foods they eat
- Other customs and traditions that people follow

  Encourage students to bring in pictures about the holiday if they have them.

 UNIT 31 The Future with *Be going to*: Statements

Unit Overview

In Unit 31 students will learn the use of *be going to* in future statements.

Grammar in Context (pages 242–243)

Comprehension Questions

- Where are Laura and Ken going? *(to a soccer game)*
- Who's playing? *(Sam, Laura's brother)*
- Is it going to rain? *(no)*
- What is the most popular game in the world? *(soccer)*

Words

- For the names of the sports, ask students to raise their hands if they like to (a) watch this sport, (b) play this sport. If there is time, ask students why they like these sports.
- Ask students what Laura means when she says "You don't have to be a giant." (In this context, a *giant* means very tall or very big.)
- Ask students questions about speed limits, e.g.: "What is the speed limit in the town where you live? What is it in the students' countries? Is it a good idea to have a speed limit? Why or why not?"

Expressions

- Students may ask why we say <u>*do the speed limit*</u>. Point out that it's also correct to say *drive the speed limit*. Elicit other idioms with *do*, e.g., "do homework, do the dishes," etc.
- Ask students which word has the same meaning as *how come*. (*why*)
- *Chill out* is an idiom used mainly by young people in the United States. Sometimes it is shortened to *chill*.

Working Together

In Part B, students who are not interested in sports may not be able to answer. Prepare a few other questions to elicit the future, e.g.: *Where is the next Olympics going to be? Are you going to watch any sports on television next weekend?*

Grammar Presentation (pages 244–245)

Identify the Grammar

- *We're going to be late.*
- *I think they're going to win.*
- *It's not going to rain.*
- *The game's going to start soon.*
- *We're going to make it on time.*

Grammar Charts

- While reading the examples on the board and in the charts, model the pronunciation that is accepted in the community where you teach. In North America *going to* is almost always pronounced *gonna*.
- To help students notice the grammar, ask questions such as the following:
  - —Which forms of *be* can we use with *going to*? *(all forms: am, is, are, was, were, etc.)*
  - —How do we form the negative of *be going to*? *(place not after the form of be)*
  - —Which kind of word comes after *to*? *(base form of the verb)*
  - —Which time expressions can we use with *be going to*? *(soon, this afternoon, tonight, tomorrow, today, later, any specific future time)*

Grammar Notes

Notes 1–4   *(Exercises 2–3)*

- You may wish to explain that *be going to* is used most often to make predictions and to talk about planned actions (as opposed to *will*).
- In the following exercises, encourage students to use contracted forms.
- Model the target grammar by pretending you are a fortune teller. Call up a student and pretend to tell his or her fortune. For example:
  - —You're going to be the first female president of your country.
  - —You're going to win a million dollars in the lottery.
- Next, write a variety of singular and plural nouns on the board. Include names of athletes and sports teams known to the students, as well as other subjects students may enjoy talking about. Have the students make affirmative predictions.
- Model negative predictions. Have students make negative predictions about the subjects you wrote on the board.
- To model the use of *be going to* for planned actions, show a page from a planner or make a list of activities you plan to do the next day or on the weekend. Model sentences about your planned activities. For example:
  - —Saturday morning I'm going to work in my garden.
  - —I'm going to have lunch with my mother on Sunday.
- Go around the room and have each student make one sentence about something they are planning to do the following day, next weekend, etc. Alternately, pick one day and time, e.g., Friday evening, and have everyone say what they're going to do at that time.

Focused Practice (pages 245–246)

Exercise 1

heavy coat: a coat suitable for very cold weather

graduate: to finish your education and receive your degree

Exercise 3

Before doing the exercise, have students identify the sport in each picture (skiing, basketball, running or track, horse racing).

Communication Practice (page 247)

Exercise 5

- Before listening, have students read the title, look at the picture, and read the items. Ask students which player is probably Laura's brother *(the one who is about to kick the ball)*.
- If necessary, explain terms related to soccer such as *goal* and *score*.

Exercise 6

If your class is large, or your students have trouble concentrating, you can do this activity in groups of six or seven.

Further Practice

In this activity[1] students make predictions about the future of objects. Bring in a set of objects, or make a list. Ingredients for foods, objects that can be combined to form new objects, objects with multiple uses, containers, and recyclable materials will work well, for example, an egg, a nail, a button, an avocado pit or some other kind of seed, a box, a bottle, a plastic container, a piece of wire, a torn piece of clothing. Put students in groups. Display the objects so that the whole class can see them, or give one or more objects to each group.

Model sentences with *be going to* using one object as an example. For instance:
- Object: an apple
- Uses: It's going to be part of a pie. / It's going to go in my daughter's lunch. / It's going to be in a fruit salad. / I'm going to eat it as a snack.

---

[1] Based on "Future of an object" from Penny Ur, *Grammar Practice Activities* (Cambridge: Cambridge University Press, 1988), page 111.

Reading the sports page. Bring in copies of the sports section from a local newspaper. Students will read to find out about an event they want to attend. (Note: You can also bring in the television listings, and have students look for a sports program they want to watch.) Put students in pairs. Distribute the newspapers. Instruct the students to work together to find articles or announcements about local sports events. Their task is to choose one event they would like to attend together. They should note the day, time, and location of the event. Have each pair of students report on the event they chose. For example:

• There's going to be a tennis tournament at the university on Sunday at 3 P.M.
• We're going to attend a soccer game at Rancho Park on Saturday morning.

UNIT 32 The Future with *Be going to: Yes / No* Questions

Unit Overview

In Unit 32 students will learn how to ask and answer future questions with *be going to*.

Grammar in Context (pages 248–249)

Comprehension Questions

• What are the speakers doing? *(eating dinner)*
• How was Tim's day? *(not bad)*
• Who called Jessica? *(a TV producer)*
• What did he want? *(He wanted Jessica to be in a new TV show.)*
• What is Jessica's new job going to be? *(the main reporter)*
• Is the show going to start soon? *(no)*

Words

• You may need to explain that a *producer* is the person who manages the business aspects of a television show or movie. For example, the producer arranges the financing, hires the actors, etc. (The director is the person who oversees the filming of the show or movie.)

• *National TV* means a show that is broadcast all over the United States. There are also local stations in most cities.
• A *big part* means a major or starring role in a television show, movie, or play.

Expressions

• Try to elicit paraphrases or explanations of the expressions. For example:
  —*Not bad:* pretty good, OK, normal, typical.
  —*(some interesting) news:* something new to tell you.
  —*As a matter of fact:* This expression is a signal that the speaker has a surprising or unexpected answer to a question.
  —*all very new:* This implies that the speaker does not know all the facts about a new situation and needs more time to get used to it.
• Initiate parallel dialogues in which you ask a question and students answer using the expressions. For example:
  —T: How was school yesterday?
    S: Not bad.
  —T: What's up?
    S: I have some interesting news.
  —T: Did your boyfriend ask you to marry him?
    S: As a matter of fact, yes.
  —T: How do you like your new school?
    S: I don't know yet. It's all very new.

Working Together

• Model a few questions, making sure to pronounce *going to* as *gonna.*
• Have students ask you the questions. Model the short answers.
• After students work in pairs, select one pair to say each dialogue in front of the class.

Grammar Presentation (page 250)

Identify the Grammar

• <u>*Are you going to have*</u> a big part?
• <u>*Is it going to mean*</u> a lot of travel?

Grammar Charts

- Write the example sentences on the board.
- Have students look at the charts and the examples on the board and ask:
  - What is the word order for *yes / no* questions with *be going to*? *(be + subject + going to + verb)*
  - Are the short answers the same as those for the simple present or those for the present progressive? *(present progressive)*

Grammar Notes

Note 1   *(Exercises 2–3)*

- Drill the form of questions with *be going to* as follows: Write a verb phrase on the board, e.g., *eat dinner with parents*. Say different nouns and pronouns and have students form the questions. For example:

  —T: have dinner with parents / you

  Ss: Are you going to have dinner with your parents?

  —T: Carla and Juan

  Ss: Are Carla and Juan going to have dinner with their parents?

- After students have practiced making questions with all possible subjects, substitute a different verb phrase and repeat. Keep changing the verb phrase in order to maintain a lively pace.

Note 2

- Review the forms of the negative short answer with *you, he, she, it, we,* and *they.* Drill by asking questions and having students answer in two ways. Be sure to ask questions that can logically take a *no* answer. For example:

  —T: Is it going to snow tomorrow?

  S1: No, it isn't.

  S2: No, it's not.

  —T: I'm studying Japanese. Am I going to speak perfect Japanese next week?

  S1: No, you aren't.

  S2: No, you're not.

- Use the questions from Working Together to ask and answer questions about students in the class. Short answers may be affirmative or negative. Model two or three questions and have students answer. For example:

  —T: Is Svetlana going to graduate this year?

  SVETLANA'S PARTNER: Yes, she is.

  —T: Is Mohammed going to buy a house?

  MOHAMMED'S PARTNER: No, he's not.

- Call on students to form the questions.

Focused Practice (pages 250–252)

Exercise 1

off: not working

Exercise 2

I'm afraid so: (spoken) used in order to politely tell someone something that may annoy, upset, or disappoint him or her.

weather channel: a television channel that mainly broadcasts information about weather

tofu: a soft white food that is made from soybeans

veggie burger: a food similar in shape to a hamburger but made without meat

Exercise 3

earn: to get money for work you do

Exercise 4

date book: a personal planner, calendar, or appointment book

Communication Practice (pages 253–254)

Exercise 5

Have students read the directions and the questions before listening. Ask inference questions. For example:

- What is the relationship between Amanda and Josh? *(They are married.)*
- Are they going to have a baby? *(yes)*
- Is it expensive to raise a child? *(yes)*
- Who is Jason, probably? *(For example: Josh's friend, boss, co-worker, neighbor, or male relative.)*

Exercise 6

Extend by having pairs of students role-play conversations between a fortune teller and a client. Bring in props and costumes if possible.

Exercise 7

Vary the exercise by having only two students take the role of mayor and director, respectively, and having the whole class interview the students. For the interview with the mayor, pretend that the other students are newspaper reporters at a press conference. For the interview with the director, the context could be a group of students who are deciding whether to re-enroll at the school or continue their studies at a different school.

Exercise 8

If necessary, you can prompt by pointing to the picture and asking a few questions such as:
- What are they (the young man and woman in the convertible) going to do? *(play tennis)*
- What's the police officer going to do? *(write a ticket for parking illegally)*

Further Practice

In this activity, students will decide whether to keep or throw away items as part of an imaginary cleaning of a messy room. Do an Internet image search for "messy room." Print out three or four different pictures or cartoons. Put students in groups of three or four. Each student gets a different picture of a messy room. Tell students to pretend that this is their room, and their classmates are going to help them clean it up. Students take turns showing the picture of their room to the group. The classmates ask questions, and the "owner" of the room answers. For example:

S1: Are you going to keep this pizza box or throw it away?

S2: I'm going to throw it away.

S3: Are you going to make the bed?

S2: No, I'm going to wash the sheets.

S4: Are you going to keep this old couch?

S2: Yes I am. It's really comfortable.

GRAMMAR OUT OF THE BOX ......

Storytelling. In this activity students will read a story that has been divided into sections. At the end of each section they will stop and make predictions about what is going to happen next. Choose a narrative that can be divided into sections. It can be fiction, such as a folktale or myth, or nonfiction of the "true stories in the news" type. Cut the story into parts. Paste each part on a sheet of paper. Write one or more *yes / no* questions with *be going to* for each section and paste them at the bottom of the page for the corresponding section. Staple all the pages of the story together. Put students in small groups and give them the cut-up story. Instruct them to read each part of the story and answer the questions about what is going to happen next. Then, as they read the next part, they can see if their predictions were correct. At the end, ask the class if their predictions were correct or if the ending surprised them.

Unit Overview

In Unit 33 students will learn how to ask and answer *wh-* questions with *be going to*.

Grammar in Context (pages 255–256)

Comprehension Questions
- How does Mark feel? *(nervous)*
- What does he ask Kathy? *(Will you marry me?)*
- Does Kathy accept? *(yes)*
- What are all the friends going to do on Sunday evening? *(watch the big game)*

Words

Ask students what happens when a couple gets engaged in their culture. For example, does the man give the woman a ring?

Expressions

Provide the following background on each of the expressions:
- *What's bothering you?* In this expression, *bother* means to worry someone. A paraphrase would be *Are you worried about something?*
- *Will you marry me?* This is the traditional formula used when a man asks a woman to marry him. It is not correct to say *Are you going to marry me?*
- *What took you so long?* This expression implies that the speaker is impatient.
- *By the way:* This expression, which learners of English often use incorrectly, is used to signal a digression or a change of topic. It is never used to open a conversation.
- *Congratulations!* This expression is said to a person who has just delivered good news about an accomplishment, award, or happy life event.

Working Together
Part B

Model the activity with a student. Have a student ask you the questions, and model both the *yes* and *no* answers. Then have two students continue modeling, with one of them asking questions and the other one answering.

Grammar Presentation (page 257)

Identify the Grammar
- *How am I going to say this?*
- *What are you going to do on Sunday evening?*
- *What time is the party going to start?*

Grammar Charts
- Ask students the following questions:
  —What is the word order in future questions that ask about the subject? *(Who / What + is / are + going to + verb)*
  —What is the word order in other future questions? *(wh- word + am / is / are + subject + going to + verb)*
- Have students follow the "formulas" above to compose original questions with *how, when, what* and subject-pattern questions with *who, what*. For example:
  —What is she going to do?
  —What is going to happen?

Grammar Notes

Notes 1–2 *(Exercise 2)*
Write the following words on the board: *who, what, when, where, why,* and *how*. Put students in pairs. Have them ask each other questions about their plans for the coming weekend with the words on the board. Model the activity with a student. For example:

T: Where are you going to go this weekend?

S: To a basketball game.

T: Who is going to go with you?

S: My brother.

→ For additional practice, see the Supplementary Activities on page 92.

Focused Practice (pages 257–259)

Exercise 2
big bucks: (spoken) a lot of money
eventually: at last; after a long time

Communication Practice (pages 259–260)

Exercise 4
Josh and Amanda are going to host a party. Have students try to predict some *wh-* questions with *be going to* that they might ask each other as they prepare.

Exercise 5
An alternative way to do this activity is to have students work in pairs and interview each other. Then put two pairs of students together to form a group of four. Each student reports what his or her partner said.

Exercise 6
- Before playing the game, identify the people in the picture. (In the car, Jessica and Tim Olson, who are taking the others to the airport. In the center, Mary Beck [Jessica's mother] and Annie and Ben Olson. Behind them Bill Beck [Jessica's father] and Jeremy Olson.) Have students read the captions. Ask them if they know where Disney World is. Remind the students that the Olsons live in Seattle.
- A variation of the game is to turn it into an information gap activity. Have students close their books or cover up the flight information at the bottom of the page.
- Instruct the class to write genuine questions about the Olsons' travel plans. Have students write their questions on the board.
- Put students in pairs or small groups. At a signal from you, have them open their books or uncover the information at the bottom of the page. The first pair or group to find the answers to all the questions on the board is the winner.

Further Practice
Have students sit in small groups and talk about (a) what they're going to do during their next vacation, or (b) what they plan to do after the end of this English course. Group members should take turns telling about their plans. The others should ask at least one question each with *who, where, when, how long,* and *what*. For example:
- What are you going to do?
- Where are you going to study?
- How long are you going to stay in Mexico?
- Who are you going to travel with?

GRAMMAR OUT OF THE BOX......

Freeze frame. Bring in a video of a half-hour comedy or drama program that your students enjoy. You can play all or part of the program. Be sure to preview it! Plan at least four places where you can stop the show so that students can predict what is going to happen. Write a number of *wh-* questions with *be going to* to ask students at those stopping points.

Introduce the program by telling students about the characters and providing other necessary background to help them understand what they are going to see. Show the program. Stop it at the places you had planned. Ask students the questions. Alternately, have the students themselves compose questions to ask. After students have discussed the questions, play the next part of the program. At the end, ask the students if their predictions were correct and if the end of the program surprised them.

Supplementary Activities

Unit 1   Notes 1–4

• Use a transformation drill to practice the three uses of the imperative. Use gestures to make the activity more fun. Use a thumbs-up to elicit the affirmative, a thumbs-down for the negative, and a hands-together (prayer) gesture for a request. Follow this sequence:

T: Tell me the answer [accompanied by prayer gesture]

Ss: Please tell me the answer.

T: [Makes thumbs-down gesture]

Ss: Please don't tell me the answer.

T: [Makes thumbs-up gesture]

Ss: Tell me the answer.

• After a few rounds, provide only a prompt and have a student come up before the class and do the gestures. For example:

T: Open your book.

S: [Makes prayer gesture]

Ss: Please open your book.

Unit 4   Note 4

In these activities students can review possessive adjectives and related spelling problems.
• Oral drill: Provide a kernel sentence. Use a variety of subject pronouns and possessive adjectives. A student follows up with an original sentence containing a possessive adjective. (Note: Some sentences can be negative.) Examples:

T: We are at school.

S: Our school is in Los Angeles.

T: My dog is not a girl (female).

S: His name is Bozo.

• Dictation: Make up short sentences with *your / you're, it's / its, their / they're,* and new or difficult vocabulary from this lesson. Examples:
—You're late. Your dinner is cold.
—It's a beautiful wallet. Its color is unusual.
—Their children are young. They're not in school.

Unit 9   Note 2

Teach students the three pronunciations of the third-person singular *-s* and *-es* endings.
• Explain that pronunciation and writing are different in English. We write *-s* or *-es*, but we say /s/, /z/, or /ɪz/.
• Put the chart on the next page on the board, a transparency, or a handout. Say the words slowly. Draw out the endings so that students can hear them clearly.

- Students from most countries have difficulty pronouncing the /z/. To teach it, instruct students to put their hands on their throats and say a few vowels: /a/, /e/, /u/, etc. They should feel vibration in their throats. Do the same thing with some voiced consonants such as /d/, /l/, /v/, /j/. Next, tell students to say /s/ with their hands on their throats. They will not feel any vibration. The final step is to add vibration, thereby producing a /z/ sound.
- Say the words with /z/ and /ɪz/ endings and have students repeat.
- Students will want to know which words take which ending. Tell students to put their hands on their throats again. Pronounce the words in the left column. Tell students to focus on the last sound and ask them if they feel vibration. They will not. Since there is no vibration with /s/, they are ready to understand that voiceless ("no vibration") sounds at the end of a verb are followed by /s/.
- Next, explain that all words that end in voiced sounds ("with vibration") are followed by the voiced /z/ except for the voiced sounds in the last column. They are exceptions.

/s/	/z/	/ɪz/
stop	need	kiss
kick	learn	teach
eat	sing	wash
laugh	fall	box
	remember	fizz
	play	
	go	
	do	

Unit 13   Notes 4–5

Mixer with *Do you ever . . . ? How often?*
- Create a handout like the one below. The first item is an example. Use any verb phrases that apply to your class.

Activity	Name	How often?
forget to take out your contact lenses at night	Linda	sometimes

- Instruct students to get up, walk around, and interview their classmates. First they should ask a question with *Do you ever . . . ?* and the verb phrases on the handout. If their classmate answers *yes*, they should then ask *How often do you. . . . ?* They should record their classmate's name and answer in the appropriate columns.
- As a follow-up, ask the class to make true statements about each student based on the information they collected. For example:

T: What did you learn about Glenda?

S1: She often has cereal for dinner.

S2: She usually does her homework before dinner.

S3: She rarely writes letters.

Unit 15   Notes 1–3

Plan a set of activities that make noise. They can be simple actions, such as opening a door, or they can involve tools or objects that you bring to class, such as a coffee grinder.

• Instruct students to put their heads down on their desks or cover their eyes.
• Do the activities. The students' task is to ask *yes / no* questions until they figure out what you are doing. For example:
  —Are you opening a drawer?
  —Are you eating potato chips?
  —Are you opening a soda can?
  —Are you cutting paper?
• If vocabulary is a challenge, you can prepare a word list and go over it with students ahead of time. However, this will spoil some of the surprise, so try to plan actions that use words the students know.

Unit 18   Note 6

• Put students in small groups and give each group a name or number. In each group there should be a secretary or recorder. That student should write the group name or number at the top of a piece of paper.
• The group should make a list of at least five foods that have not been mentioned yet in the lesson. The list should include count nouns in plural form and non-count nouns.
• Collect the papers. Shuffle them and redistribute, making sure no group gets its own paper.
• Group members should look at the list of foods they received, and each student should say whether he or she likes or dislikes the foods on the list.

Unit 22   Notes 1, 5

Bingo
• Create Bingo cards with 9 boxes as in Unit 21, Further Practice. Fill in the squares with a mix of regular and irregular verbs in the base form. (For irregular verbs, see Grammar Note 5.)
• For each verb you write on the Bingo cards, write the same verb on a strip of paper. Put all the strips in a box or hat.
• To play the game, draw strips out of the hat and say the verbs in the base form. Instruct students to write the past form on their cards.
• A student who has three filled-in boxes in a row (horizontally, vertically, or diagonally) should call out "Bingo!"
• Check the student's card by having him or her read both the base and the past forms of the verbs.
• Continue playing as time permits.

Unit 25   Notes 1, 3–4

An Auction
Conduct a class auction. You will need play money and a variety of interesting or silly items. Follow these steps:
• Put all the items in a large bag and distribute the play money. As you conduct the auction, students should be able to see only one item at a time.
• Pull the items out of the bag one by one. As you show the class each item, ask, "How much for this (beautiful lamp)?"

- Students should answer by stating dollar amounts, e.g., "Five dollars/Six-fifty," etc.
- As soon as there is a lull in the bidding, say, "(Dollar amount) going once, going twice, SOLD to the (lady in the yellow shirt) for (dollar amount)."
- "Give" the item to the "purchaser" and collect payment from him or her.
- Students can continue bidding only as long as they have money.
- When all the items have been "sold," students can offer to "buy" items from one another. Write useful expressions on the board, such as,
  —*How much do you want for that bracelet?*
  —*How much for the bottle of perfume?*

Unit 30   Notes 1–3

Make a Date

The purpose of this activity is for students to find a time when they can go to a movie together.

- If students have planners, tell them to bring their planners to class. If they don't have planners, make copies of a blank planner page. Pass them out and have students fill in all the times they are busy during the coming week.
- Put students in pairs. Tell them they cannot look at their partner's planner.
- Students should ask each other questions until they find a time that is convenient for both of them. For example:

S1: Are you free on Thursday evening?

S2: Sorry, no. I have to study for a test that night. How about Saturday in the afternoon?

S1: I have a hair appointment at 3 P.M. I'm free after that.

- Have students report the day and time they agreed upon.

Unit 33   Notes 1–2

Interview

Have students pretend to interview a famous person who has come to the end of a project or a stage of his or her career, such as a president at the end of his or her term, an actor who has just won an Oscar, a scientist who has won the Nobel Prize, and so on.

- Tell students the name of the person they're going to interview and what that person has just accomplished. Instruct them to write at least three questions with *be going to*. They can be *yes / no* questions or *wh-* questions. For example:
  —What are you going to do next?
  —Are you going to write another book?
  —How are you going to spend your time after you retire?
  —When is your next movie going to appear?
- Select one student to play the role of the famous person.
- Have the class interview him or her.
- An alternative to this activity is to bring in a guest speaker and have the class interview the guest about his or her work and future plans.

Audioscript

Unit 1

Exercise 7 (page 7)

STEVE: The homework is on the board. Read pages 1 to 10 and study the words on page 9.

MARK: Is that all?

STEVE: No. Answer the questions on page 10. Don't answer question 8. The answer is too long. That's it. See you tomorrow.

Unit 2

Exercise 5 (page 14)

1. **STEVE:** This is my mother, Mary Beck. She's here at the university today.

   MARK: Hello, Mrs. Beck. I'm Mark Mason.

2. **STEVE:** These are my posters. They're from different countries.

   JUDY: They're wonderful.

   STEVE: Thanks.

3. **STEVE:** This is my sister.

   MARK: It's a good photo.

   STEVE: Thanks.

4. **STEVE:** These are our tickets.

   PEDRO: Are they for tonight?

   STEVE: Yes.

5. **MARY:** This is my husband, Bill.

   MARK: Hi, Bill. It's nice to meet you.

   BILL: It's nice to meet you too.

Unit 3

Exercise 7 (page 24)

AMY: Hello, I'm Amy Beck.

MATTEO: Nice to meet you. I'm Matteo Milano.

AMY: Nice to meet you. Are you from around here?

MATTEO: No, I'm from Italy. What about you?

AMY: I'm from Australia, but my parents are from Italy.

MATTEO: Oh, really? Are you a student?

AMY: Yes, I am. What about you?

MATTEO: I'm a chef.

Unit 4

Exercise 4 (page 30)

A.

1. **JOSH:** Who's that woman over there?

   MARK: That's my grandmother from Nashville.

2. **JUDY:** Do you know those men, Steve?

   STEVE: Yes. They're my friends from the university.

3. **STEVE:** Are those your parents, Judy?

   JUDY: Yes, they are. And that's my brother Ken with them.

4. **AMY:** Jenny, where's my purse?

   JENNY: It's in the bathroom, Amy.

5. **ANNIE:** It's your turn to do the dishes, Ben.

   BEN: No, it's not. It's your turn, Annie.

6. **TIM:** Jessica, where are my keys?

   JESSICA: They're on the table, Tim.

Exercise 6 (page 31)

A: Are those your children?

B: Yes. They're our sons, Jeremy and Ben. And that's our daughter, Annie.

A: And is that their dog?

B: Yes. His name is Bozo.

A: Who are those other kids?

B: Those are their friends.

Unit 5

Exercise 5 (page 37)

1. **A:** Who's that woman with Amanda?

   B: Her name is Kathy.

   A: Is she married?

   B: No, she's not.

2. A: Is he your brother?

    B: Yes, he is.

    A: Is he a writer?

    B: No, he's not. He's a doctor.

Exercise 7 (page 37)

A: This is a nice wedding.

B: It sure is. Say, who's that woman?

A: That's my friend Susan. She's a writer.

B: Is she married?

A: No, she's single.

B: Oh. And who are those guys?

A: They're my cousins, Bobby and Mike. They're brothers.

B: Who's *that* woman?

A: That's my wife, Laura.

B: She looks nice.

A: She is.

Unit 6

Exercise 4 (page 44)

MAN: Excuse me. Is this Main Street?

WOMAN: Yes, it is. We're on Main Street near Second Avenue.

MAN: I'm looking for the post office. Is it on Main Street?

WOMAN: No, it's not. It's on First Avenue.

MAN: Oh. Where's First Avenue?

WOMAN: Walk to the corner of this street. Turn right at the corner. The post office is next to the bank. It's on the corner of First and Washington.

Exercise 6 (page 45)

MAN: Excuse me. Where's the nearest supermarket?

WOMAN: It's on the northeast corner of Washington Street and First Avenue. This is Washington Street and Second Avenue. Walk down Washington one block. The supermarket is across from the bank.

MAN: Thanks. One more thing. Do they sell flowers in that supermarket?

WOMAN: Uh, yes, they do. But walk down Second Avenue one block and there's a big flower shop on the northeast corner of Main and Second. The flowers there are beautiful.

MAN: Thanks.

Unit 7

Exercise 5 (page 54)

MARK: Hello. This is Mark. Sorry I can't take your call right now. Please leave a message.

JOSH: Hi, Mark. This is Josh. Hey, where were you last night? Amanda and I were at the movies. We saw *Spider-Man 3*. It was really interesting. It was exciting too. Call me, OK? Bye.

Unit 8

Exercise 5 (page 60)

MARK: Hey, Jason. How are you? How was your weekend?

JASON: It was great.

MARK: Where were you?

JASON: At the beach.

MARK: How was the weather?

JASON: Nice. It was sunny and hot.

Unit 9

Exercise 6 (page 71)

MAN: Is anyone sitting here?

TIM: No. Have a seat, please.

MAN: Oh! I'm really tired. . . . Are you going to Seattle?

TIM: Yes, I am. You too?

MAN: Yes. When do we get to Seattle?

TIM: Let's see . . . About 7:30 tonight, I think. . . . Are you from around here?

MAN: Actually, I'm not. I come from Romania. I live in Bucharest.

TIM: Romania? Hmm. Your English is really good. I don't speak any languages besides English. Just a little Spanish.

MAN: Thank you.

TIM: Do people speak English in Romania?

MAN: A lot of people know some English. Some people speak it. My family is different. Everyone speaks three languages.

TIM: Really?

MAN: Yes, my parents worked at the United Nations. So we speak English, French, and Romanian, of course.

Exercise 7 (page 72)

Tim: Do you live in Seattle?

Man: For the moment. My wife has a teaching job at the university this year.

Tim: Oh. What does she teach?

Man: She teaches European literature. She also writes novels.

Tim: That sounds interesting.

Man: Yes, it is. But it's also difficult. She doesn't speak American English too well. What about you? What do you do?

Tim: I'm a graphic artist. I work for an advertising agency.

Man: And do you live in Seattle?

Tim: We don't live *in* the city, but we live *near* it.

Unit 10

Exercise 7 (page 80)

Judy: Are you going to the game?

Mark: No. It's my grandmother's birthday and I need to get a gift. Do you have any ideas?

Judy: Let's see. Does she like music?

Mark: I don't know.

Judy: Well, does she like to read?

Mark: I don't really know.

Judy: Does she like chocolate?

Mark: I think so. But I'm not sure.

Judy: I've got it. I know the perfect gift.

Mark: You do? What?

Judy: Spend the day with her.

Mark: That's not a gift.

Judy: Yes, it is. Your time is a gift. I'm sure she'll love it.

Unit 11

Exercise 5 (page 87)

Margaret: Excuse me. Is anyone sitting here?

Jason: No. Sit down, please.

Margaret: Are you new here?

Jason: Yes. Today's my first day on the job.

Margaret: Oh. Welcome to the company. My name's Margaret Boyd.

Jason: Nice to meet you, Margaret. I'm Jason Mendoza.

Margaret: Nice to meet you too, Jason. What do you do?

Jason: I'm an accountant. What about you?

Margaret: I'm a writer. I write advertisements for the company.

Jason: Oh. That's interesting. Well, this is a good company, I think. The only problem is the traffic. I live in Belmont. It takes more than an hour to get here.

Margaret: Really? I live in Belmont too. But I take the bus—it's usually about half an hour.

Jason: That sounds good. Where do you catch the bus?

Margaret: At Tenth and Maple.

Jason: Really? I live near there.

Margaret: Why don't you take the bus tomorrow? I catch the eight o'clock bus.

Jason: Great idea. See you then.

Unit 12

Exercise 4 (page 94)

A: He's very good looking.

B: Thanks. I agree. He has a cute mustache.

A: Is he a musician?

B: Yes, he is. He's a jazz pianist.

A: He looks tall. About how tall is he?

B: Almost 6 feet tall. He's tall and thin and his fingers are very long.

A: Yes, they are. He has a nice smile. Tell me. How old is he?

B: My grandfather is 65 years old.

Unit 13

Exercise 5 (page 101)

Ken: Hello?

Grandma: Hi, Kenny. How's my favorite grandson? And happy birthday.

Ken: Oh, hi, Grandma. Thanks a lot. But it's not until tomorrow.

Grandma: I know. But I'm usually early. So how are you?

Ken: Well, pretty good, but . . .

Grandma: But what?

Ken: Well, I'm always tired. I have a new job, and . . .

Grandma: That's good. But why are you tired so much? Are you eating your vegetables? Getting enough sleep?

Ken: Well, maybe I have too much to do. I usually start work at 1:30, and I never have time for lunch.

GRANDMA: Kenny! No! You have to eat lunch. And what about sleep?

KEN: Well, sometimes I stay up late to study.

GRANDMA: How much sleep are you getting?

KEN: Usually about five or six hours.

GRANDMA: Kenny! That's not enough.

KEN: I know, Grandma, but . . .

GRANDMA: But nothing. You need to take a lunch with you to work. And you need to get eight hours of sleep every night.

KEN: Well . . .

GRANDMA: Promise me.

KEN: OK, Grandma.

Unit 14

Exercise 5 (page 112)

JEREMY: Hi, guys. How's it going?

ANNIE: OK.

BEN: Fine.

JEREMY: Busy?

ANNIE: Well, I'm writing a story.

BEN: And I'm watching TV.

JEREMY: Too bad. I have tickets to a rap concert.

ANNIE: Tickets to a rap concert? OK. I'm finished. I'm not writing anymore.

BEN: And I'm not watching TV.

JEREMY: Well, come on. Let's go. The concert is in 20 minutes. Just one thing . . .

ANNIE: What?

JEREMY: Don't tell Mom and Dad about our school reports. Wait a week.

BEN AND ANNIE: No problem.

Exercise 7 (page 113)

ANNIE: Is Dad home?

BEN: Yes. He's in the living room. He's reading the paper.

ANNIE: Where's Mom?

BEN: She's in the office. She's answering her e-mail.

ANNIE: Is anyone else home?

BEN: Grandpa is. Grandma's outside. She's gardening.

ANNIE: What's Grandpa doing?

BEN: He's cooking.

ANNIE: Grandpa's cooking?

BEN: Well, actually he's baking. He's making a carrot cake for Grandma.

ANNIE: Oh, that's so sweet.

Unit 15

Exercise 3 (page 118)

KELLY: Hello.

SUSAN: Kelly? It's me, Susan. So, tell me. Is Jeremy there?

KELLY: Uh . . . sure. Right here with me.

SUSAN: Oh, you're so lucky. Are you watching TV together?

KELLY: Yeah. We're watching a video.

SUSAN: Are you watching a romance?

KELLY: Uh-huh. We're watching *Sleepless in Seattle*.

SUSAN: Awesome. Is Jeremy wearing his cool basketball jacket?

KELLY: Sure. And he wants to take me to a concert.

SUSAN: Wow!

KELLY: Hey, Susan, I'm kidding. Jeremy isn't sitting here with me. We're not watching a video together. He isn't even here. Jeremy and his uncle are watching a silly basketball game. And—Jeremy doesn't even know I exist.

Exercise 6 (page 120)

STEVE: Hello.

JESSICA: Hi, Steve.

STEVE: Jessica! Hi. How are you?

JESSICA: Great. How about you? How are you doing?

STEVE: Busy. Very busy. I'm teaching three new courses and writing articles for the *Daily Times*.

JESSICA: Boy, you *are* busy. Try to relax. Listen. Thanks again for the games for Ben.

STEVE: Is Ben really enjoying them?

JESSICA: He loves them.

STEVE: I'm glad. How's Annie?

JESSICA: Great. Guess what she's doing?

STEVE: I don't know. Is she acting in a school play?

JESSICA: No.

STEVE: Is she playing soccer?

JESSICA: No. She's writing for her school paper!

STEVE: That's my girl. Now I know she's a Beck.

JESSICA: Come for dinner this weekend. We miss you.

STEVE: I'm too busy this weekend, but next weekend, I promise.

JESSICA: All right. Bye, little brother.

STEVE: Bye, big sister.

Unit 16

Exercise 6 (page 127)

ANNIE: Hi, Dad. What are you doing?

TIM: Hi, Annie. I'm fixing the TV.

ANNIE: Is it broken?

TIM: No, I'm just fixing the color.

ANNIE: Oh. Is Jeremy taking a shower?

TIM: Yes.

ANNIE: Again? Why is Jeremy taking another shower?

TIM: He has a date later.

ANNIE: Oh, so that's why. Is Mom making dinner?

TIM: Yes, she is.

ANNIE: What's she making?

TIM: Her specialty: chicken and rice.

ANNIE: Oh, great. I love chicken and rice. Are Grandpa and Grandma coming?

TIM: Yes, they are. They're here. Uncle Steve is here too.

ANNIE: Oh. What's Uncle Steve doing?

TIM: He's sleeping on the sofa in the living room.

ANNIE: Why is he sleeping now?

TIM: He was up late last night.

ANNIE: Oh. Is he OK?

TIM: Well, he's not feeling well.

Unit 17

Exercise 5 (page 136)

1. That's my mother's magazine.
2. My father's car is across from the restaurant.
3. Those are their children's CDs.
4. That's my boss's office.
5. Are these your roommate's glasses?
6. No, they're Chris's glasses.

Exercise 7 (page 137)

JUDY: So how did dinner with Kathy's parents go?

MARK: It went well, I think. Her dad's a really nice guy.

JUDY: What did you talk about?

MARK: His boat. That's his passion.

JUDY: Do you know anything about boats?

MARK: A bit. My friend's dad has a boat and I'm often invited.

JUDY: That's good. And what's Kathy's mom like?

MARK: She seemed nice too, but she was quiet. Kathy's aunt, her mom's sister, is in the hospital. I think Kathy's mom was worried about her.

JUDY: Is she very sick?

MARK: No, but Kathy's mom is still worried.

JUDY: I can understand. Did anyone say anything about your goatee?

MARK: Kathy did. She doesn't like it. She misses my beard.

JUDY: Oh, well.

MARK: But she liked my tie and suspenders.

JUDY: I guess you'll have to grow back your beard and keep borrowing your roommate's clothes.

Unit 18

Exercise 5 (page 145)

WAITER: May I help you?

MARK: Yes. Can we order lunch?

WAITER: I'm sorry. We serve lunch at 11:00. It's only 10:30. How about a snack?

JUDY: Well, all right. Some chips and salsa for me, and a cup of coffee, please.

WAITER: I'm sorry. The coffee machine is broken.

JUDY: Broken? Well, how about tea?

WAITER: All right. What kind?

JUDY: Iced tea.

WAITER: Sorry, no iced tea. All we have is hot tea.

JUDY: OK. A cup of hot tea and chips and salsa.

WAITER: I'm sorry, ma'am, but we're out of salsa. I can bring you some chips . . . And for you, sir?

MARK: Some mineral water, please.

WAITER: Sorry, sir. We don't have any mineral water. All we have is lime soda. Or regular water.

MARK: Hmm. OK. Lime soda, please.

WAITER: All right, sir. There's just one thing. The soda isn't cold.

MARK: No kidding!

JUDY: I can't believe this place!

Unit 19

Exercise 2 (page 149)

1. **A:** What do you want for your birthday, Mary?

   B: I want a good novel. And I want an umbrella—a red one.

2. A: Annie, is someone at the door?

   B: Yes, there's a man outside. He's an old man.

3. A: Grandma, I have an interview tomorrow.

   B: Oh, good, Ken. I hope it's a good interview.

Exercise 5 (page 151)

JOSH: Amanda, let's go out tonight.

AMANDA: Sure. What do you want to do?

JOSH: Let's go to a concert. There are two or three good ones.

AMANDA: Great. But, Josh, what about the dog?

JOSH: Let's take him to my Mom's. She wants to see him.

AMANDA: OK. Hey, here's an idea. Let's take her a photograph of the house.

JOSH: Good idea. How about this one?

AMANDA: Fine. OK, let's go . . . Uh-oh. It's raining. Bring an umbrella.

JOSH: OK. The big one or the small one?

AMANDA: The big one.

JOSH: It's still in the car.

AMANDA: OK. Let's go.

Unit 20

Exercise 2 (page 157)

KATHY: Mark, this is Mei Liang. She was lost in the park. She was very, very, upset. She can't speak a word of English.

MARK: Oh? Poor kid!

KATHY: Mark, you can speak a little Chinese. Can you help her?

MARK: Well, let me see. I hope she can understand Mandarin. Uh . . . She lives with her grandmother.

KATHY: That's good to know. Can she remember her grandma's number?

MARK: She can't remember the number, but her grandmother's name is Li Li Wang and they live in Kent.

OFFICER: I'm looking it up in the phone book . . . We've got her number. Thank you. Can you two wait for her grandmother?

MARK: Sure.

OFFICER: Her grandmother is on the way. She's really upset.

Exercise 4 (page 158)

1. A: We can't hear you.

   B: Sorry. Is that better?

2. A: We can hear you.

   B: That's good.

3. A: I can't believe it.

   B: It's true.

4. A: I can believe it.

   B: Well, I can't.

5. A: I can't see the board.

   B: Then change your seat.

6. A: I can see the board.

   B: Good. Please read the sentence on the board.

Unit 21

Exercise 5 (page 168)

1. ANNE: Hi, Judy. This is Anne. Thanks for the flowers. They arrived yesterday, just in time for my birthday. They're beautiful.

2. MARK: Hi, Judy. This is Mark. I'm still at work. I finished my report last night, but I still have calls to make. Let's meet at 7:00, not 6:00.

3. AMANDA: Hi, Judy. This is Amanda. Josh and I watched a really good movie on TV a couple of days ago. It's on again tonight. Watch Channel 6 at 8 o'clock. Don't miss it.

Exercise 6 (page 168)

1. He graduated from college last year.

2. They started a business 10 years ago.

3. They worked for 10 hours yesterday.

4. They hired many people last month.

5. They learned a lot last year.

6. A company wanted to buy their business three years ago.

7. They agreed to the sale yesterday afternoon.

Unit 22

Exercise 5 (page 175)

TEACHER: Class, today we're interviewing Yoshio Tanaka. Yoshio is our exchange student at Redmond High this year. Everybody ready? Who has the first question?

STUDENT 1: I do. Yoshio, when did you come to the United States?

YOSHIO: I came in July. That was four months ago.

TEACHER: OK. Next question?

STUDENT 2: Where are you from in Japan, Yoshio? Tokyo?

YOSHIO: Well, I was born in Tokyo, but my family moved to Hamamatsu when I was four. It's a city south of Tokyo.

STUDENT 3: Did you play sports in high school?

YOSHIO: Yes, I did. I played soccer. But my favorite sport was karate. I did karate for a long time, and I got a black belt.

STUDENT 1: Wow! . . . What else did you do when you were in school?

YOSHIO: Mountain climbing. I climbed Mt. Fuji when I was 14.

STUDENT 2: Why did you want to be an exchange student?

YOSHIO: Well, my family and I took a trip to the United States when I was 10. We went to a lot of places—New York, Los Angeles, Florida. After that I always wanted to come back.

STUDENT 3: Did you visit Seattle on that trip?

YOSHIO: No, we didn't. But I always wanted to come to Seattle.

STUDENT 1: Do you like it here?

YOSHIO: Yes, I really do. Everyone is friendly. And I love the water and the mountains.

Unit 23

Exercise 4 (page 181)

B.

1. **A:** They arrived late.
   B: When did they arrive?

2. **A:** They arrived at 2 A.M.
   B: *When* did they arrive?

3. **A:** She got there by horse.
   B: *How* did she get there?

4. **A:** She got there late. Her car didn't start.
   B: How did she get there?

5. **A:** I'm leaving for Alaska.
   B: *What* did you say?

6. **A:** I'm leaving for home.
   B: What did you say?

7. **A:** The president came to my house.
   B: *Who* came to your house?

8. **A:** The letter carrier came to my house.
   B: Who came to your house?

Exercise 6 (page 182)

AMANDA: Hi, Rob.

ROB: Hey, Amanda. How's it going?

AMANDA: Good. How's everything with you? What did Dad say about the car?

ROB: Well, at first he was pretty angry. But then I promised to pay for the damage.

AMANDA: You did? How can you do that?

ROB: I got a part-time job. I'm a cashier at BG Drugstore.

AMANDA: Great. When did you start?

ROB: A couple of days ago. It's not bad.

AMANDA: What are your hours?

ROB: They're different on different days. Yesterday I worked from 9:00 to 5:00. The day before I worked from 9:00 to 12:00.

AMANDA: How's the pay?

ROB: So-so. But it's a job.

Unit 24

Exercise 5 (page 192)

TIM: Oh, no! Jessica! I need help.

JESSICA: What's the matter?

TIM: I wrapped all the gifts. But who are they for? I don't remember.

JESSICA: Well, let's see. What's in the long, red box?

TIM: A tennis racquet.

JESSICA: So that's for your cousin Martha, right?

TIM: Yeah, that's right. It's for her.

JESSICA: OK. Now what's in the small green box?

TIM: Let me think . . . Oh, I remember. A CD.

JESSICA: Is it for Steve?

TIM: No, it's not jazz. It's a CD of a Broadway musical.

JESSICA: Oh. So it's for Mom and Dad.

TIM: Yeah, right. It's for them.

JESSICA: So what about Jeremy?

TIM: Uh . . . oh, yeah. It's the orange box. It's a DVD.

JESSICA: Good. Now, what about this big, white box? What's in it?

TIM: Um . . . oh, yeah. It's a game. Ben and Annie love games.

JESSICA: Right. OK. Now . . . what's in this small blue box?

TIM: Don't touch that!

JESSICA: Why not?

TIM: Because it's something special.

JESSICA: Oh, I see. Is it for me?

TIM: Yep.

Unit 25

Exercise 5 (page 198)

JUDY: What are you listening to?

JOSH: The news.

JUDY: Oh. Turn it up.

NEWSCASTER: I'm Rich Williams with tonight's local news. Good evening, everyone. Last Monday travel writer John Phillips died at the age of 92. He was the author of more than 30 popular books. Phillips had four children and ten grandchildren, but in a surprise move, he left his $6 million to his assistant, his gardener, his cook, and his housekeeper. Today Phillips's lawyer, Dan Evans, read a letter dated two months ago. In it Phillips wrote, "My family spends very little time with me. They really don't know me or care about me. These four employees are my real family. Each one is a special person. I want them to have my money." Phillips's family plans to contest the will.

Unit 26

Exercise 6 (page 206)

MARTIN: Hello! Are you folks going all the way to Manchester?

JOSH: Yes, we are. You too?

MARTIN: Yes, so I guess we'll be together. It's nice that there are only four of us in the compartment—we'll have a lot of space. I'm Martin Jones, and this is my wife Helen.

JOSH: Glad to meet you. I'm Josh Wang, and this is my wife Amanda.

AMANDA: Nice to meet you.

HELEN: Nice to meet you.

MARTIN: Nice to meet you.

HELEN: You two must be from the United States. Is that right?

AMANDA: Yes, we are—from Seattle, Washington. I suppose you can tell by our accent.

HELEN: Yes. Actually, you both have very nice accents.

JOSH: Thanks. We *love* the British accent. But you know, there *are* a few differences between British and American English.

MARTIN: Yes? What, for example?

JOSH: Well, for one thing, you say "biscuits" here. When you have tea in your room, you have biscuits with it. And here you say "Underground."

HELEN: What do you call those things in America?

AMANDA: We call biscuits cookies. We call an Underground a subway, or maybe a metro.

MARTIN: Is there an Underground in Seattle?

AMANDA: No, there isn't. There's a small monorail.

JOSH: You know, here's a question. We stayed in a bed-and-breakfast in London and really liked it. Do you two know of a good one in Manchester?

HELEN: Well, there are two nice ones near the train station.

JOSH: That's great. Where . . .

Unit 27

Exercise 3 (page 214)

CLARA: So, Jill. How was your date?

JILL: OK. We met at 11:00 in front of the coffee shop. I had blueberry pancakes. They were delicious. He just drank a glass of orange juice. I guess he wasn't hungry.

CLARA: What did you talk about?

JILL: School mostly. He's a math major. He plans to teach.

CLARA: What did he wear?

JILL: He wore a light blue shirt and jeans.

CLARA: Are you going to go out again?

JILL: I don't know. He was nice and polite.

Exercise 5 (page 215)

BRIAN: Hey, Ken, how's it going?

KEN: Fine, man. What's up?

BRIAN: Well, I borrowed some CDs from Mia Klein. I want to return them, but I'm too busy today. Can you give them to her? She's in your history class.

KEN: Sure, but I don't know her. What does Mia look like?

BRIAN: Oh, she's very tall and thin. She has long dark hair. She usually wears jeans, a black turtleneck, and interesting earrings. She's cute, but she never smiles. She's very serious.

KEN: Oh. I think I know her.

BRIAN: Good. Thanks a lot.

KEN: No problem.

Unit 28

Exercise 5 (page 224)

GRANDMA: Hello?

KEN: Hi, Grandma. This is your favorite grandson. How's my favorite grandma?

GRANDMA: Kenny! What a nice surprise. How are you doing? What are you up to?

KEN: Well, I'm pretty busy. My classes are harder than they were last semester. I'm taking chemistry and physics.

GRANDMA: How are you doing?

KEN: OK. The thing is, I have a problem about next term. I can take art or music. I love music, but the music teacher is very tough. I'm not very good at art, but the art teacher is really cool. Her tests are a lot easier than the music teacher's. She gives less homework and higher grades. So, what do you think?

GRANDMA: I say, take the art class. I remember you were very good at art as a child.

KEN: Hmm. Maybe you're right. A good teacher makes a big difference. So, how are you? Is everything OK?

GRANDMA: Yes, dear. I'm doing just fine. Today my reading group is coming here. I'm making my strawberry cheesecake.

KEN: They're lucky. . . . Well . . . I guess you're pretty busy, so I'll let you go. Anyway, it's almost time for me to go to work. Talk to you soon, Grandma.

GRANDMA: Yes. Bye, Kenny. Thanks for calling.

Unit 29

Exercise 4 (page 230)

JOSH: This is my newest stamp; it's from Egypt. I bought it in London. And this is my favorite stamp. It's from Italy. It's the most valuable one in my collection.

MARK: Not this one?

JOSH: No, not this one. This one is from Brazil. It's the biggest stamp, but not the most valuable.

KATHY: Where's this stamp from?

JOSH: Austria. It's the oldest one in my collection. It's from the year 1906.

MARK: That's about a hundred years old. Isn't it very valuable?

JOSH: No, not really.

KATHY: This one is beautiful.

JOSH: I agree. It's the most artistic one of all. It's from Korea.

KATHY: This one is also very nice.

JOSH: Yes, it is. It's from Switzerland. Of all my stamps, it's the most colorful.

Unit 30

Exercise 5 (page 237)

AGENT: World Airlines. How may I help you?

FELIX: I'd like to make a reservation for a flight to Bucharest, Romania. My name is Felix Maxa.

AGENT: Yes, Mr. Maxa. When would you like to leave?

FELIX: On Thursday, January 30th.

AGENT: There's a flight leaving Seattle at noon on Thursday, with a connecting flight in New York. It's a direct flight from New York to Bucharest, leaving at 10:30 P.M. and arriving in Bucharest at 5:05 P.M. the next afternoon.

FELIX: Are there any other options?

AGENT: Yes, there's another flight leaving Seattle at 6:30 in the evening, arriving in New York at 2:30 A.M. But there's no direct flight to Bucharest until 10:00 the next morning.

FELIX: I think the noon flight is better.

AGENT: OK. Is this one-way or round trip?

FELIX: Round trip. I'd like to be back in Seattle on Friday, February 7th.

AGENT: All right, Mr. Maxa. How would you like to pay for that? [trails off]

Unit 31

Exercise 5 (page 247)

KEN: Hey, this is pretty exciting after all.

LAURA: I told you.

KEN: Yeah, you did. But look at those clouds. I still think it's going to rain.

LAURA: Don't worry. It's not going to rain. Take my word for it.

KEN: Hmm. OK . . . The score's 2–2. Do you still think Sam's team is going to win?

LAURA: I think so. Hey, Sam's going to take a penalty kick.

KEN: So what does that mean?

LAURA: He's going to kick the ball. If it goes in, his team wins.

KEN: Wow! That was pretty cool! He did it.

LAURA: I told you. So do you want to go to another soccer game sometime?

KEN: Well, sure!

Unit 32

Exercise 5 (page 253)

Josh: Hello.

Amanda: Hi, Josh. It's me.

Josh: Hi, Amanda. How are you? What did the doctor say?

Amanda: I'm fine.

Josh: Great.

Amanda: And I have some wonderful news. I was right. Josh, we're going to be parents next July!

Josh: Oh . . . my . . . gosh! I can't believe it! That's pretty soon.

Amanda: Well, in seven months or so you're going to be a daddy.

Josh: That's terrific!

Amanda: Listen, Josh. I have to go back to work now. See you tonight.

Josh: Bye, honey. Take care. I love you.

Amanda: I love you too.

[Later]

Josh: Hey guys. I'm going to be a father!

Jason: Congratulations! Are you going to move?

Josh: Are you kidding? Not right away. We're not going to buy a house for a few years.

Jason: Is Amanda going to stay home with the baby?

Josh: Only for the first three months. Then her mom's going to watch the baby. Her mom's great with kids.

Jason: That's terrific, but did you know it's going to cost $200,000 to raise a child born next year?

Josh: Well, are you guys going to start a collection for me?

Unit 33

Exercise 4 (page 259)

Josh: Amanda, what are we going to eat?

Amanda: When?

Josh: At the party on Sunday night—when people come over to watch the game.

Amanda: Let's have pizza. And . . . let's have milk to drink.

Josh: Milk? Why are we going to have milk?

Amanda: Just kidding! Let's have soda.

Josh: Sounds good. Now what time are we going to have dinner?

Amanda: Well, when is the game going to start?

Josh: Six, I think.

Amanda: OK, let's have dinner about 5:30.

Josh: Good. Now who's going to call the people?

Amanda: You are.

Josh: Me? Everybody?

Amanda: Just kidding! Why don't you call the men, and I'll call the women?

Josh: All right.

Student Book Answer Key

NOTE: Where a short form or contracted form is given, the full or long form is also correct (unless the purpose of the exercise is to practice the short or contracted forms).

UNIT 1 Imperatives   (pages 2–8)

Working Together
Mark's route: From the spot at "You are here" to the corner of Fifth and Jackson, left on Jackson, down Jackson to Third, right on Third, stop.

Write an "X" on the restaurant on the corner of Jackson and Third.

1

_d_ **2.** Don't park there.
_a_ **3.** My hands are full.
_b_ **4.** Don't turn left.

2

2. Make a U-turn.
3. Don't park here.
4. Turn right.

3

2. Listen to this CD.
3. Close the window, please.
4. Don't read this book.
5. Please don't smoke.
6. Please turn to page 6.

4

     Don't   *door*
1. A ~~Do not~~ (open) the ~~window~~.
    Don't open the door.
    Please don't   *garage*
2. B ~~Do not~~ park in the ~~driveway~~.
    Please don't park in the garage.

5

2. don't sit   **3.** Don't park   **4.** open   **5.** Listen

6

   Don't
2. ~~You no~~ sit here.
   Please study OR *Study page 3, please.*
3. ~~Study please~~ page 3.
   Complete
4. ~~Completes~~ the sentences.
   Please don't OR *Don't worry, please.*
5. ~~Don't please~~ worry.
   Don't
6. ~~No~~ close the window.

7

B. 10 (ten)
the words / 9 (nine)
Answer the / 10 (ten).
Don't answer / 8 (eight)

9

A. a

UNIT 2 *This is / These are*; Subject Pronouns   (pages 9–14)

1

2. d   **3.** f   **4.** c   **5.** a   **6.** e

2

2. This   **5.** This   **7.** this
3. These   **6.** These   **8.** these
4. This

3

2. They   **4.** you   **6.** They   **8.** We
3. It   **5.** I   **7.** I   **9.** he

4

These
2. A: ~~This~~ are my brothers.
   B: Hello. Nice to meet you both.

         is
3. A: This ^ my partner, Ahmed.
   B: Hi, Ahmed.

      Are
4. A: ~~Is~~ these your books?

         they're
   B: No, ~~they~~ not.

5

A. 1. This   **2.** These   **3.** This   **4.** These   **5.** This

UNIT 3 The Present of *Be*: Statements
(pages 18–24)

1

2. A   **3.** A   **4.** N   **5.** N

2

2. They are   **3.** It is   **4.** We are   **5.** He is

3

A. *Answers to 2, 3, 5, 8, and 9 may vary.*
2. ✓ OR I am not a new student.
3. ✓ OR My parents are not in Australia.
4. The Sydney Opera House is not in Canberra.
5. ✓ OR We are not in room 2.
6. Mexico is not the capital of Mexico City.
7. ✓
8. ✓ OR My parents are not from around here.
9. ✓ OR It is not hot here.

4

2. 're not   **4.** 's   **6.** are   **8.** is   **10.** 're
3. 're   **5.** 's not   **7.** 's   **9.** 's   **11.** are

5

2. 'm not   **4.** 're   **6.** 's not OR isn't
3. 're   **5.** 's not OR isn't

6

                 not
1. B: It's ~~no~~ cold. It's hot.

               'm
2. A: Please open the window. I ~~be~~ hot.

            It's
   B: Hot? It's not hot. ~~Is~~ cold.

            's
3. A: My cousin ^ from Tokyo. She's a student.

            's
   B: My cousin ^ from New York. She's a student too.

4. A: Seattle is the capital of Washington.

            it
   B: No, ~~it's~~ isn't. Olympia is the capital.

7

1. True   **5.** No Information
2. False   **4.** No Information
3. True

UNIT 4 *That is / Those are;* Possessive Adjectives; Plural Nouns
(pages 25–31)

1

d **1.** Are those <u>your</u> (books)?
e **2.** Is that <u>his</u> (school)?
b **3.** Are those <u>your</u> (children)?
c **4.** Is that the EMP?
f **5.** Is that <u>your</u> (college)?
a **6.** Are those <u>your</u> (stadiums)?

a. Yes. One is for football. The other is for baseball.
b. Yes. <u>Their</u> (names) are Judy and Ken.
c. Yes. <u>Its</u> (shape) is unusual, right?
d. No, they're <u>her</u> (books).
e. No, it's <u>my</u> (school).
f. No, I go to Boston College.

2

2. those   **4.** Those   **6.** those
3. that   **5.** that

3

2. our   **4.** his   **6.** his
3. their   **5.** Its   **7.** her

4

2. men   **4.** purse   **6.** keys
3. parents **5.** dishes

5

they're
1. **B:** No, ~~they~~ her keys.

daughter
2. **A:** That is my ~~daughters~~.

woman
B: She's a beautiful ~~women~~.

those   *children*
3. **A:** Are ~~that~~ your ~~childs~~?
B: Yes. That's our son, and that's our daughter.

its
4. **A:** Are ~~it~~ tires flat?
B: Yes, they are.

6

1. your	**5.** our	**9.** is
2. children	**6.** daughter	**10.** those
3. our	**7.** their	**11.** their
4. sons	**8.** His	

UNIT 5 The Present of *Be*: *Yes / No* Questions, Questions with *Who* and *What* (pages 32–38)

Working Together
B. 2. a mechanic   **3.** a nurse   **4.** a cashier

1

Questions with *Be*:

Are you here for the wedding?

Is Mark single?

Are you and Josh friends?

Short Answers:

Yes, I am.

Yes, he is.

Yes, we are.

2

2. d   **3.** e   **4.** f   **5.** a   **6.** b

3

2. What	**4.** Who	**6.** What
3. Who	**5.** What	

4

2. **A:** Is the game today?
B: Yes, it is.
3. **A:** Are they cousins?
B: No, they aren't. They're brothers.
4. **A:** Who is that man?
B: He's my teacher.
5. **A:** Is Seattle hot?
B: No, it isn't.

5

1. **A:** Is she
B: No, she's not.
2. **A:** Is he
B: Yes . . . is
A: a writer
B: No . . . not. He's a doctor.

6

I am
1. **B:** Yes, ~~I'm~~.
2. **A:** Is she single?

she's
B: No, ~~she~~ not.

Are they
3. **A:** ~~They~~ students?

aren't
B: No, they ~~are~~.
4. **A:** Is he your father?

not
B: No, he's ˄

Is
5. **A:** ~~Are~~ your car new?

it's
B: No, ~~it~~ old.
6. **A:** Is he an engineer?

he's   *He's*
B: No, ~~he~~ not. ~~He~~ a writer.

7

1. No, she's not. OR No, she isn't.
2. No, she's not. OR No, she isn't.
3. Yes, they are.
4. No, she's not. OR No, she isn't.

UNIT 6 The Present of *Be*: Questions with *Where*; Prepositions of Place (pages 39–45)

Working Together

10 First Avenue

1

2. c **3.** b

2

2. on First **3.** 10 First Avenue **4.** on the second

3

2. d **3.** c **4.** a

4

A. MAN: I'm looking for the post office. <u>Is it on Main Street?</u>

MAN: Oh. <u>Where's First Avenue?</u>

WOMAN: Walk to the corner of this street. <u>Turn right at the corner.</u>

C. The man and the woman are on Main Street, just north of Second Avenue.

5

1. A: Where ^{'s} Bogotá?

   B: It's ~~on~~ ⁱⁿ Colombia.

2. A: Is your apartment ~~in~~ ^{on} this floor?

   B: No, it's on the ~~eight~~ ^{eighth} floor.

3. B: It's ^{on} First Avenue.

   A: Is it next ^{to} the museum?

4. A: Is the supermarket on First ~~in~~ ^{between} Main and Washington?

6

The supermarket is the unmarked building on the northeast corner of Washington and First.

The flower shop is the building at the corner of Main Street and Second Avenue.

UNIT 7 The Past of *Be*: Statements, *Yes / No* Questions (pages 49–55)

1

A.

<u>d</u> **1.** Were you at home yesterday?

<u>e</u> **2.** Was he in class yesterday?

<u>a</u> **3.** Was the concert good?

<u>f</u> **4.** Was the movie interesting?

<u>b</u> **5.** Was Susan at the library yesterday?

<u>c</u> **6.** Were you at the ball game last night?

a. No, it wasn't. The music was pretty bad.

b. Yes, she was. We were both there.

c. Yes, I was. It was a really exciting game.

d. No, I wasn't. I was at a concert.

e. No, he wasn't. He was sick.

f. Yes, it was. Johnny Depp is a great actor.

B.

Judy,

   You didn't call me last night. Where <u>were</u> you? <u>Were you</u> out? <u>I was</u> at home from 6:00 on. I tried you a couple of times. We need to talk. Please call soon.

Ken

2

2. was   **5.** was   **7.** weren't

3. Were   **6.** Were   **8.** were

4. wasn't

3

2. were at home   **5.** were at a play

3. was at a concert   **6.** was at a party

4. was at a soccer game

4

Mark,

   Sorry I ~~was~~ ^{wasn't} home last night. I ~~were~~ ^{was} at a

basketball game. Amanda and Josh ~~was~~ ^{were} with

me. It ~~were~~ ^{was} really exciting.

   Where were you on Tuesday afternoon?

Susan and Brent and I ~~are~~ ^{were} at the soccer game,

but you ~~were~~ there. Too bad. It ~~is~~ really *weren't* *was*
exciting.

 I'll talk to you soon. Call me.

 Kathy

5

1. F **2.** T **3.** F **4.** F **5.** T **6.** NI **7.** T

UNIT 8 The Past of *Be*: *Wh-*Questions

(pages 56–61)

1

b **1.** (Where) were you last
   night?
e **2.** (Who) was with you?
d **3.** (How) was the game?
c **4.** (How long) was the
   game?
a **5.** (How) was the
   weather?

a. It <u>was</u> warm.
b. I <u>was</u> at a soccer
   game.
c. Two hours.
d. Exciting.
e. My sister.

2

1. B: It was great.
2. A: Where were you?
 B: At a jazz concert.
3. A: When was the concert?
 B: It was last night.
4. A: Who was the musician?
 B: It was Wynton Marsalis.
5. A: How long was the concert?
 B: It was two hours.

3

2. Who was
3. Where was
4. When was the party
5. Who were Mark and Jason with
6. How long was

4

1. B: Saturday evening was great.
 A: Where ~~was~~ you? *were*
 B: At a soccer game.
 A: How ₐthe game ~~was~~? *was*
 B: Exciting and long.
 A: How long ~~were~~ it? *was*
 B: Three hours.

2. A: How ~~were~~ your vacation? *was*
 B: OK.
 A: Where ₐyou ~~were~~? *were*
 B: ₐ~~Was~~ at the beach. OR At the beach. *I was*
 A: How ~~were~~ the weather? *was*

5

1. b **2.** a **3.** b

UNIT 9 The Simple Present: Statements

(pages 65–73)

1

A. Check sentences 3–4, 6
B. Check sentences 2–5

2

2. Ali lives in Amman, Jordan. He speaks Arabic.
3. João and Rosa live in Salvador, Brazil. They speak Portuguese.
4. Elena lives in Santiago, Chile. She speaks Spanish.
5. Maureen and James live in Dublin, Ireland. They speak English.

3

2. wants   **5.** wants   **8.** don't want
3. don't want **6.** wants   **9.** want
4. want   **7.** wants

4

2. doesn't like, likes   **4.** doesn't want, wants
3. needs, doesn't need

5

Dear Mary,

 Spain is great. The Spanish people are very
friendly, but they ~~speaks~~ so fast. Jim ~~speak~~ *speak* *speaks*
Spanish very well. He ~~don't~~ understand *doesn't*
everything, but he ~~understand~~ a lot. I speak a *understands*
little Spanish. I don't understand much yet.

It's rainy here! People say it ~~don't~~ *doesn't* usually rain much in the summer here. We're at my cousin's house. He and his wife ~~lives~~ *live* in a beautiful apartment in Madrid. Juan ~~work~~ *works* in an office downtown. His wife Alicia ~~not works~~ *doesn't work*. She stays at home with the children.
See you soon.
Rose

6

1. b **2.** c **3.** a **4.** a **5.** c **6.** b

7

1. teaches **4.** work **7.** live
2. sounds **5.** live
3. doesn't speak **6.** don't live

UNIT 10 The Simple Present: *Yes / No* Questions (pages 74–81)

1

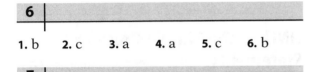

_c_ **1.** Do you know a good yoga teacher?

_a_ **2.** Do you take yoga lessons with him?

_d_ **3.** I think so. Does your cousin have classes for beginners?

_b_ **4.** Sure. Do you have a pen? My pen doesn't work.

a. Yes. He gives lessons in the park three times a week. Do you want to learn yoga?

b. No problem.

c. Yes, I do. My cousin teaches yoga. He's excellent.

d. Yes, he does. They're at 6:00 P.M. every Wednesday. Do you want his number?

2

2. Does, cost **4.** Does, live **6.** Does, have
3. Do, need **5.** Do, like **7.** Does, mean

3

2. Do you know a good Mexican restaurant?
3. Does your family eat dinner together?
4. Does your best friend live near you?
5. Do your friends like to work out?
6. Do your friends spend time at malls?

4

2. Yes, he does. **6.** No, I don't.
3. Yes, I do. **7.** Yes, she does.
4. No, she doesn't. **8.** No, they don't.
5. No, it doesn't.

5

2. Do you want **4.** Do you spell
3. Does he have time **5.** do you take

6

B: Yes, I do. It's on Main Street.
A: Does it ~~stays~~ *stay* open late?
B: Yes, it ~~do~~ *does*.
A: What's the name of the restaurant?
B: Jasmine.
A: Do you ~~spelled~~ *spell* it J-A-S-M-I-N?
B: Uh-huh, but it has an e at the end.
A: ~~Costs the restaurant~~ *Does the restaurant cost* a lot?
B: No, it ~~don't~~ *doesn't*. It's very reasonable. And it has a garden.
A: Thanks. It sounds perfect.

7

1. Do you have any ideas?
2. Does she like music?
3. does she like to read?
4. Does she like chocolate?
5. Spend the day with her.
6. Your time is a gift. I'm sure she'll love it.

UNIT 11 The Simple Present: *Wh-* Questions (pages 82–88)

1

What do you mean?
What time do you go to bed?
Who wakes you up?
How do you like your boss?
What do you talk about?

2

2. What time do you start work?
3. What do you do in your job?
4. Who do you work with?
5. How late do you stay up at night?
6. What sport do you really like?
7. Why do you like it?
8. When do you play it?

3

2. what time do you go to bed
3. how do you feel
4. why do you play soccer
5. what does *fascinating* mean
6. How do you spell *sleepy*
7. who wakes your father up in the morning

4

A: At a bookstore.

B: What ⌃do you do?   *(do inserted above ⌃)*

A: I'm a salesperson.

B: ~~Does~~ you like the work?   *(Do above)*

A: Yes. It's challenging.

B: *Challenging*? I don't know that word. What
~~means challenging~~? *(does challenging mean above)*

A: It means "hard but interesting."

5

1. Jason is (new in the company).
2. He's an accountant.
3. She's a writer.
4. Yes, he does.
5. He dislikes the traffic.
6. They live in Belmont.
7. No, she doesn't.
8. She catches the bus at 8:00.

UNIT 12 The Simple Present: *Be* and *Have*   (pages 89–95)

1

2. A, have   **5.** Q, be   **8.** Q, have
3. N, be   **6.** N, have
4. Q, have   **7.** Q, be

2

2. Where is she from?
3. Is she in Japan now?
4. Does she have any sisters or brothers?
5. Is he a violinist?
6. Does Midori have other interests?
7. What's the Midori Foundation?

3

MARK: Twenty-five.

JUDY: Where ⌃he from?   *('s above ⌃)*

MARK: São Paulo.

JUDY: Is he a writer like you?

MARK: No. He ⌃a musician. He plays the guitar.   *('s above ⌃)*

JUDY: ⌃~~He~~ cute?   *(Is he above)*

MARK: Yes, he is. He looks like me.

JUDY: Does he ~~has~~ a girlfriend?   *(have above)*

MARK: Yes, he ~~do~~.   *(does above)*

JUDY: That's too bad.

4

A

UNIT 13 Adverbs of Frequency   (pages 96–101)

1

He (always) runs . . .
(Sometimes) he feels tired . . .
He (often) has eggs . . .
. . . but (sometimes) he has cereal . . .
. . . he's (never) late.
He (rarely) stays late.
. . . Josh (sometimes) reads.
. . . (sometimes) he paints.
He's (always) in bed by 10:30.

1. **B:** Yes, I often do.
2. **A:** Are you ever tired in the morning?
   B: I'm always tired then.
3. **A:** How often do you exercise?
   B: I usually exercise five times a week.
4. **A:** What do you usually do in the evening?
   B: I often practice the piano.

3

2. Jessica never drives to work.
3. Jessica usually arrives at work on time.
4. Jessica sometimes cooks dinner.

4

DOMINGO: I exercise six or seven days a week.

JESSICA: Do ~~ever you~~ *you ever* get tired of exercising?

DOMINGO: Sure I do. But ~~always I~~ *I always* do it.

JESSICA: OK. How often do you travel?

DOMINGO: I travel a lot—at least three times a month.

JESSICA: Does ~~ever your wife~~ *your wife ever* get unhappy because you travel so much?

DOMINGO: No, ~~never she~~ *she never* gets unhappy. She ~~travels usually~~ *usually travels* with me.

JESSICA: That's great, Domingo. Now, good luck in your next game.

5

1. his birthday
2. early
3. tired
4. 1:30
5. for lunch
6. to study
7. about five or six hours
8. eight hours

UNIT 14 The Present Progressive: Statements (pages 105–114)

1

I'm wearing baggy jeans and a funny hat.
I'm playing ball with Joe.
He's not enjoying that picnic.

2

2. 's watching, 's not doing OR isn't doing
3. 're working, 're not playing OR aren't playing
4. 're making, 're not making OR aren't making
5. 'm calling, 'm not calling
6. 's driving, 's not taking OR isn't taking
7. 's raining, 's not snowing OR isn't snowing

3

2. 's sitting, is writing
3. 's eating, 's drinking
4. are playing, 're not doing OR aren't doing
5. 's wearing, is reading
6. 's sleeping

4

B. 2. F   **3.** T   **4.** F

5

2. I'm watching
3. OK. I'm finished. I'm not writing
4. I'm not watching TV
5. No problem

6

2. We ~~no are~~ *aren't OR 're not* eating pasta now.
3. They're ~~make~~ *making* chicken right now.
4. He ⌃*'s* reading the newspaper now.
5. It ~~no is~~ *isn't OR 's not* raining today.
6. I ~~no~~ *'m not* drinking water. I ⌃*'m* drinking soda.
7. She isn't ~~talk~~ *talking*. She's ~~listen~~ *listening*.
8. You ~~not~~ *'re not OR aren't* listening to me.

7

Dad	in the living room	reading the paper
Mom	in the office	answering her e-mail
Grandma	outside	gardening
Grandpa	in the kitchen	baking a carrot cake

10

Differences between the two pictures:
In Picture A

Tim Olson is cooking hot dogs.

The man with Tim Olson and Bill Beck is holding a can.

Three children (Annie, Ben, and Jeremy) are playing soccer.

Three teenagers are sitting.

The woman sitting near Jessica isn't wearing any glasses.

Mary isn't wearing a hat.

In Picture B

Tim Olson is cooking chicken.

The man isn't holding anything.

The three children are playing volleyball.

The two teenage girls are sitting, but the boy is standing.

The woman sitting near Jessica is wearing sunglasses.

Mary is wearing a hat.

UNIT 15 The Present Progressive: *Yes / No* Questions (pages 115–121)

Working Together

B. 1. c **2.** b **3.** d **4.** a

1

Check questions 3, 5, and 7.

2

2. d **3.** a **4.** b **5.** f **6.** e

3

2. We're watching a video.
3. Are you watching a romance?
4. We're watching

5. Is Jeremy wearing his cool basketball jacket?
6. I'm kidding.
7. Jeremy isn't sitting OR Jeremy's not sitting
8. We're not watching a video OR We aren't watching a video.
9. Jeremy and his uncle are watching

4

1. B: isn't. He's watching a movie.
2. A: Are you wearing a new hat?
   B: I'm not.
3. A: Is it raining?
   B: Yes, it is.
4. A: Is the baby sleeping?
   B: No, he isn't OR No, he's not.
5. A: Are they celebrating their anniversary?
   B: Yes, they are.

5

1. B: No, he ^'s not. He's playing chess.
2. A: Are you ~~wear~~ *wearing* my T-shirt?
   B: Yes, I am. Is that OK?
3. A: Is ^*it* raining?
   B: Yes, ~~it's~~ *it is*.
4. A: Are they ~~read~~ *reading* in the living room?
   B: No. They ~~read~~ *'re reading* in the bedroom.
5. A: ^*Is* Steve working hard?
   B: Yes, ~~is he~~ *he is*.
6. A: Am ^*I* sitting in the right seat?
   B: Yes, you are. You're in 7B.
7. A: Is she ~~do~~ *doing* her homework?
   B: I don't know.
8. A: Are they ~~eat~~ *eating* breakfast?
   B: I think so.
9. A: ~~He~~ *Is he* getting a haircut?
   B: I'm not sure.

6

1. Yes **2.** No Information **3.** Yes **4.** No

7

A.

DENNIS THE MENACE

shoes | a glass of milk | a sandwich
a sofa

glasses

a coat

B. *Possible answers:*

Is the babysitter sleeping?

Is Dennis sleeping?

Is Dennis's father wearing glasses?

Is Dennis eating a sandwich?

Is Dennis drinking a glass of milk?

Is Dennis wearing shoes?

Are Dennis's parents standing near the sofa?

UNIT 16 The Present Progressive: *Wh*- Questions

(pages 122–127)

Working Together

B. Ben is eating spaghetti and meatballs.

Jessica is eating pizza.

Tim is eating tacos and beans.

Jeremy is eating stew.

Annie is eating chicken and rice

1

_e_ **1.** (What) are you making?
_b_ **2.** (Who)'s playing the guitar?
_d_ **3.** (How)'s it going?
_c_ **4.** (Where)'s Jessica going?
_a_ **5.** (Why) is Dad making dinner?

2

2. Who is taking a shower?　　　　　d
3. How are you feeling this morning?　　c
4. What is Grandma making?　　　　　a

3

2. Where are Grandma and Grandpa going?
3. Who is visiting you?
4. What are you making?
5. How is your daughter doing in school?

4

1. B: He ^'s not feeling well.

2. A: Who ^'s singing in the shower?
　　B: ~~Jeremy's~~. *Jeremy is*

3. A: Why ~~you are~~ studying, Jeremy? *are you*
　　B: I have a biology test tomorrow.

4. A: Why ^are you wearing a suit today?
　　B: My other clothes are dirty.

5. A: Who ^are you talking to?
　　B: Dad. He's at the supermarket.

6. A: What ^'s she wearing?
　　B: A blue suit.

5

1. ↑　**2.** ↓　**3.** ↑　**4.** ↓　**5.** ↑　**6.** ↓　**7.** ↓　**8.** ↑

6

1. She's talking to her father.
2. He's taking a shower.
3. He has a date later.
4. She's making dinner. OR She's making her specialty. OR She's making chicken and rice.
5. He's sleeping.
6. He was up late last night.
7. He's not feeling well.

UNIT 17 Possessive Nouns; *This / That / These / Those* (pages 131–138)

1

c 1. Let's visit (Kathy's) grandmother.	a. Nice to meet you. I'm (Kathy's) friend Mark.
e 2. Are <u>those</u> your (father's) glasses?	b. What's the problem? I hope it's not the brakes again.
a 3. <u>This</u> is my (sister's) friend Melanie.	c. <u>That</u>'s a good idea. She loves visitors.
b 4. (Mark's) car is in the auto repair shop.	d. <u>That</u>'s too bad.
d 5. She has a broken leg.	e. No, they're not. They're my (mother's).

2

A. **1.** these **2.** that **3.** That, This **4.** This, these **5.** those

B. **1.** women's **2.** parents' **3.** Kathy's

3

2. Steve Beck's mother
3. Kathy White's mother
4. husband's name
5. Kathy's sister

4

2. That's too bad.
3. That's right.
4. That's a good idea.

5

2. father's, /z/
3. children's, /z/
4. boss's, /ɪz/
5. roommate's, /s/
6. Chris's, /ɪz/

6

My family loves to eat out. On my ~~parents~~ *parents'* anniversary we go to a Chinese restaurant. That's because my ~~parent's~~ *parents* love Chinese food. On my ~~brother~~ *brother's* birthday we go to an Italian restaurant. My brother loves Italian food. On my ~~sister~~ *sister's* birthday we go to a Mexican restaurant. That*'s* because her favorite food comes from Mexico. And on my birthday we go to a different restaurant every year because I like to try different places. ~~These~~ *This* year I want to try a Brazilian restaurant.

7

1. b **2.** c **3.** a **4.** c **5.** a

8

A. *Possible answers:*
In Picture B:

Hye Won is holding Juan's briefcase and is wearing Renee's sandals and Amy's belt. She is not wearing glasses.

Ari is wearing Renee's backpack and Juan's scarf, and is talking on a cell phone.

Renee is wearing Amy's hat and boots.

Amy is wearing Ari's cap and Hye Won's sandals, and is listening to Hye Won's portable sound system.

Juan is wearing Renee's scarf and Amy's glasses.

UNIT 18 Count and Non-count Nouns; *Some* and *Any* (pages 139–145)

1

Count Nouns	Non-count Nouns
some vegetables	some meat
some carrots	a piece of chicken
some peas	a slice of roast beef
some beans	a piece of pie
a salad	some fruit
an orange	a bowl of ice cream
an apple	a cup of coffee
a banana	a cup of tea

2

2. some
3. a
4. a
5. ø
6. some
7. a
8. ø
9. a slice of
10. an
11. a glass of

3

2. any soda
3. any chips
4. some fruit
5. some olives
6. some black olives
7. any green olives
8. some OR any ice cream
9. some chocolate ice cream

4

1. B: No, I don't. But I like a ~~sandwich~~. *sandwiches*
2. A: Can I bring you some coffee?
   B: No, thanks. I don't drink ~~a coffee~~. *coffee*
3. A: Are we having ~~egg~~ for lunch? *eggs*
   B: Yes, we are. We're also having a yogurt.
4. A: Does the plant need water?
   B: No, it doesn't need ~~some~~ water. *any*

5

1. F, The restaurant isn't serving lunch now.
2. T
3. F, The restaurant doesn't have iced tea.
4. NI
5. T
6. F, The restaurant doesn't have mineral water.
7. NI
8. F, Mark and Judy don't like the restaurant.

UNIT 19 *A / An and The; One / Ones* (pages 146–152)

1

1. B. a hat in general   **3. B.** cars in general
2. A. one   **4. A.** all of the jackets
2. B. one   **4. B.** one red jacket
3. A. a car in general

2

2. an   **3.** a   **4.** a   **5.** an   **6.** an   **7.** a

3

2. The   **3.** the   **4.** the   **5.** the   **6.** an

4

Dear Kathy,
   Josh and I have ~~an~~ great house! ~~House~~ is *a*   *The house*
very big, but it's also ~~a~~ old one. It needs work. *an*

It has ~~the~~ nice living room, but the colors are *a*
terrible. Each wall is ~~the~~ different color. There's *a*
~~a~~ orange wall, ~~an~~ yellow wall, a blue wall, and *an*   *a*
~~the~~ red wall. We need to repaint. *a*
   We want you to see ~~a~~ house. Give me ~~the~~ *the*   *a*
call.

Love,
   Amanda

5

1. more than one   **4.** one
2. one   **5.** more than one
3. more than one   **6.** one

7

Possible answers:

I see an old woman carrying an open umbrella. She is talking to a mannequin.

I see a salesman eating a pizza.

I see an old man with a cat on a leash.

I see a woman wearing shoes with different colors.

I see a man wearing socks with different colors.

I see a girl wearing a woman's hat. The hat is on backwards.

I see a boy trying on a very big blazer.

UNIT 20 *Can / Can't* (pages 153–159)

1

Sentences with *can* and *can't*:
How can you do it?
We can try all of them.
Request: Can I speak with Ms. White?

2

2. you can speak a little Chinese.
3. Can you help her?
4. Can she remember her grandma's number?
5. Can you two wait for her grandmother?

3

~~speak~~
2. Mei Liang Wang can't ~~speaks~~ English. She can ~~to~~ speak Mandarin Chinese.

3. Mei Liang is a good ice skater. She can
   skate
   ~~skates~~ very well.

   can
4. Mei Liang ⌃sing well, but she can't ~~not~~ dance.

4

A.
1. can't	3. can't	5. can't
2. can	4. can	6. can

B.
1. can't	3. can't	5. can't
2. can	4. can	6. can

UNIT 21 The Simple Past: Regular Verbs (Statements) (pages 163–169)

Working Together
B. convention, stayed, Grand, listened, presentation

1

A. started, worked, hired, fired, learned, offered, agreed, ended up, used
B. start, work, hire, fire, learn, offer, agree, end up, use

2

2. graduated	4. stayed	6. opened
3. worked	5. learned	

3

2. stayed	6. didn't rain
3. cleaned	7. didn't stay
4. watched	8. didn't clean
5. didn't play	9. played

4

2. Hi, Ted. This is Al. I ~~am~~ arrived this morning. My phone number is 345-9090.

   Yesterday OR I talked to Ellen yesterday.
3. Hello, Ted. This is Melissa. ⌃I ~~yesterday~~ talked to Ellen. She loved your speech.

4. Hi, Ted. This is Judy. Sorry I ~~was~~ missed your call. Call me. I have some exciting news.

   This morning OR I received your gift this morning.
5. Hi, Uncle Ted. This is Mark. ⌃I received ~~this morning~~ your gift. It's awesome. Thank you so much. I love the game.

5

Message from	
1. Anne	flowers, yesterday
2. Mark	at work, 7:00, 6:00
3. Amanda	watched, movie, days ago, 8, 6

6 Pronunciation

Sentence	Base Verb	/t/	/d/	/ɪd/
1. He graduated from college last year.	graduate			✓
2. They started a business 10 years ago.	start			✓
3. They worked for 10 hours yesterday.	work	✓		
4. They hired many people last month.	hire		✓	
5. They learned a lot last year.	learn		✓	
6. A company wanted to buy their business three years ago.	want			✓
7. They agreed to the sale yesterday afternoon.	agree		✓	

UNIT 22 The Simple Past: Regular and Irregular Verbs; *Yes / No* Questions (pages 170–176)

1

Yes / No questions in the simple past:
Did you eat anything this morning?
Did you stay up late last night?
Irregular verbs: drank, had, had, went, got

2

2. got up	7. left	12. went
3. was	8. took	13. didn't have
4. didn't take	9. arrived	14. didn't leave
5. ate	10. saw	15. got
6. drank	11. wasn't	

3

2. did you and Amanda get up
3. did it rain
4. Did Jeremy go
5. Did I call
6. Did your parents leave

4

Dear Rose,

   Greetings from beautiful Jamaica! Thanks for taking us to the airport. Our flight

didn't leave
~~not leave~~ until 1 P.M., so the plane didn't

   arrive   *were*
~~arrived~~ until 10:30. We ~~was~~ really tired when

   got   *was*
we ~~get~~ to the hotel. But that ~~is~~ two days ago. Now the sun is shining and it's warm.

                     went
   Yesterday we ~~go~~ swimming at the beach. I

bought
~~buy~~ some great gifts for people. Today we

   slept
~~sleeped~~ until 9:30!

   Hope everything is OK in Seattle. Is it cold?
Love,
   Mary

5

1. Yes	4. Yes	7. No
2. No	5. Yes	8. No
3. No Information	6. No	9. Yes

UNIT 23 The Simple Past:
Wh- Questions   (pages 177–183)

Working Together
B. 1. He had a car accident.
   2. It happened in front of a video store.
   3. It happened this morning.
   4. He didn't want to go to his father's auto repair shop.

1

What time did you see him?

What did he look like?

What did he say?

2

2. Why did you drive there
3. what happened
4. How long did the drive take
5. What did your parents say

3

2. Who ate sushi last night
3. Who taught you to ride a bicycle
4. Who came late today
5. Who visited you last weekend
6. Who gave you a special gift last year

4

B. 2. surprise	**6.** information
3. surprise	**7.** surprise
4. information	**8.** information
5. surprise	

5

A: At 9:30 this morning.

                    happen
B: Where did it ~~happened~~?

A: It happened on Oak Street between First and Second Avenues.

        did it
B: How ~~it did~~ happen?

A: A cat ran into the street. The car ahead of me stopped suddenly, and I hit it.

B: Thank you for reporting the accident.

          did
C: What ʌ the insurance company say?

A: Nothing. Just "Thank you for reporting the accident."

6

1. He promised to pay for the damage. OR The damage.
2. He started work a couple of days ago. OR A couple of days ago.
3. He worked eight hours. OR Eight hours.
4. He worked three hours. OR Three hours.

UNIT 24 Subject and Object Pronouns (pages 187–192)

1

STEVE: Well, <u>we</u>'re having a party on Sunday at my apartment. <u>You</u> and Josh are both invited. Are <u>you</u> free at three o'clock?

AMANDA: <u>I</u> think so. What's the occasion?

STEVE: <u>It</u>'s Jessica's birthday, but <u>I</u> don't know what to get. What's a good gift? Any ideas?

AMANDA: How about some CDs? Does <u>she</u> like music?

STEVE: Yes. <u>She</u> listens to (it) all the time.

AMANDA: Good. Get (her) some CDs. Now, tell (me) again. What's your new address?

STEVE: 14 Vine Street, Apartment 202.

AMANDA: OK. See (you) then.

2

1. B. She	**4. A.** them	**6. A.** They
2. B. he, him	**4. B.** They	**6. B.** them
3. A. you, us	**5. A.** it	
3. B. you	**5. B.** it	

3

1. Why don't you get them a travel book?
2. Why don't you get her a tennis racquet?
3. Why don't you get him a vest?
4. Why don't you get me a DVD?

4

Dear Sarah,

Jim and ~~me~~ *I* are having a party on Saturday, June 10, at 3:00. ~~Is~~ *It's* for our son, Bob, and our daughter, Sally. ~~They~~ *Their* birthdays are both in June. You and Stan are invited.

Please don't bring ~~they~~ *them* any presents. ~~Are~~ *We're* just having a band and lots of food, but no gifts. Please come! Give John and ~~I~~ *me* a call if you can come.

See you soon,
Doris

5

Color of Box	Who is it for?	Gift
red	Cousin Martha	*a tennis racquet*
green	Mom and Dad	*a CD*
orange	Jeremy	*a DVD*
white	Ben and Annie	*a game*
blue	Jessica	*something special*

UNIT 25 *How much / How many; Quantity Expressions* (pages 193–199)

1

2. 10 days.
3. A lot.
4. 12 people.
5. Two, Quito and the Galápagos Islands.

2

2. c **3.** e **4.** a **5.** d

3

2. How many days is it? OR How many days is the trip?
3. How many meals do they provide? OR How many meals does the trip include?
4. How many people to a room? OR How many people share a room?

4

2. **A:** How many ~~book~~ *books* do you read in a month?
   B: Not ~~much~~ *many*.
3. **A:** How much time do you spend online?
   B: Not ~~many~~ *much* time.
4. **A:** How ~~much~~ *many* trips do you take in a year?
   B: Two or three.

5

A. and B.

1. How many / He wrote more than 30 travel books.
2. How many / He had 4 children.
3. How many / He had 10 grandchildren.
4. How much / He had $6 million.

5. How many / He left his money to four people—his assistant, his gardener, his cook, and his housekeeper.

6. How much / His children spent very little time with him.

UNIT 26 *There is / There are*

(pages 200–206)

1

JOSH: Thank you. We're glad <u>there's</u> a room for us.

MRS. BRADY: Actually, <u>there are</u> two rooms to choose from, one on the second floor and one on the third. The one on the third floor <u>has</u> a nice view, but <u>there isn't</u> an elevator, unfortunately.

AMANDA: Oh, that's fine. We'd like the one with the nice view. <u>Is there</u> a bath in the room?

MRS. BRADY: No, <u>there isn't</u>. Sorry about that. <u>There's</u> just one bathroom per floor. But we don't have many guests. So, let's see . . . breakfast goes from 7:00 until 9:00. <u>There's</u> tea in your room, and <u>there are</u> also some nice biscuits. Your room is up that stairway over there. We'll see you in the morning.

JOSH: Thanks a lot. See you then.

2

2. there is
3. there's
4. Are there
5. there's
6. there are
7. They're

3

2. how much rain is there
3. how much snow is there
4. how many theaters are there

4

2. there   3. It   4. There   5. There   6. They

5

Dear Kathy,
   Greetings from London! We're having a
There are
wonderful time. ~~It's~~ so many interesting things
There
to see and do here! ~~They~~ are interesting little
there are
shops on every street, and ~~there's~~ lots of fun
things to buy. I hope my suitcase is big enough.
There
~~They~~ are also a lot of great museums; we went
to the Tower of London yesterday, and we're
going to the British Museum today. We're
staying at a really nice bed-and-breakfast.
It's   *there*
~~There's~~ a nice, comfortable place, and ~~they~~ are
lots of interesting people from different
countries staying here.
   I have to sign off now; we're ready to go to
the museum. Say hi to Mark and everyone else.
Love,
Amanda

6

1. There are two other people in Josh and Amanda's compartment.
2. There are a few differences between British and American English.
3. The American word for *biscuits* is *cookies*.
4. The American word for *Underground* is *subway* or *metro*.
5. No, there isn't (an Underground in Seattle). (OR No, there's no Underground in Seattle.)
6. Yes, there is (a monorail in Seattle).
7. There are two nice bed-and-breakfasts near the train station in Manchester.

UNIT 27 **Noun and Adjective Modifiers**

(pages 210–217)

1

c 1. He's a (biology)
a 2. He likes to take <u>long</u>
f 3. We are listening to a (jazz)
b 4. They have <u>similar</u>
d 5. He likes to read (grammar)
e 6. Let's meet in front of the (gift)
i 7. She's a <u>famous</u> (movie)

_g_ **8.** My <u>favorite</u> dish is (chicken)
_j_ **9.** They both like <u>modern</u>
_h_ **10.** He always wears (cotton)

2

2. Marty is older than Ken.
3. Ken's clothes are more colorful than Marty's clothes. OR Ken's clothes are more colorful than Marty's.
4. Laura is shorter than Mi Young.
5. Mi Young's hair is darker than Laura's hair. OR Mi Young' s hair is darker than Laura's.
6. Lisa is better than David
7. Maia is worse than Jason

2

2. black cotton T-shirts
3. baggy jeans
4. a black sports car
5. small brick house
6. beautiful rock garden

3

3. blueberry
4. pancakes
5. delicious
6. orange
7. juice
8. hungry
9. math
10. major
11. blue
12. nice
13. polite

3

1. B: I think cafeteria food is worse.
2. A: Are you taller than your father?
   B: Yes, but he's heavier.
3. A: Is Paris more interesting than Marseilles? OR Is Marseilles more interesting than Paris?
   B: Yes, but it's more expensive.
4. A: Which is better, *War of the Worlds* or *Cinderella Man*? OR Which is better, *Cinderella Man* or *War of the Worlds*?
   B: I think *War of the Worlds* is better.

4

Dear Dahlia,
   My boyfriend, Joe, is wonderful. He's ~~a~~ kind,
                    a good
honest, and intelligent. He has ~~an~~ job ~~good~~ and
        heart
a ~~heart~~ kind. There's only one problem. He
doesn't like to spend money. We always watch
                          cable
TV at his house, and he doesn't even have TV
                    free
~~cable~~. Sometimes we go to ~~frees~~ concerts and
picnics. I have fun with Joe, but I want to do
 different
~~differents~~ things. Do you have any suggestions?
Sincerely,
Rosa

4

Dogs Rule
                              better
   In my opinion, a dog is a ~~gooder~~ pet than a
cat. I know because we have a dog and a cat at
home. Here are my reasons. First, a dog is
 friendlier   *happier*
~~friendly~~ than a cat. My dog is ~~more happy~~ to
see me when I come home. My cat just doesn't
                      more active
care. Second, a dog is ~~activer~~. I always take my
dog for a walk. I can't do that with my cat.
She only wants to sleep. Third, a dog is more
interesting than a cat. My dog is a lot more
            than
playful ~~that~~ my cat. He knows a lot of tricks.
My cat doesn't know any tricks at all. She's a
     more   *protective*
lot boring. Last, a dog is more ~~protectiver~~ than
a cat. My dog barks if anyone comes to the
house. The cat just runs and hides. I think dogs
rule.

5

Mia is the third woman from the left.

5

1. F **2.** NI **3.** T **4.** T

6

1. b **2.** f **3.** a **4.** d **5.** c **6.** e

UNIT 28 Comparative Adjectives (pages 218–224)

1

A.

Short Adjectives	Adjectives That End in -y	Long Adjectives	Irregular Adjective Forms
older	easier	more interesting	worse
quicker	funnier		better
cheaper			
faster			
smarter			

UNIT 29 Superlative Adjectives

(pages 225–231)

1

A. the prettiest
the most beautiful
the most expensive

B.

Adjective	Comparative Adjective	Superlative Adjective
scary	scarier	the scariest
cold	colder	the coldest
quick	quicker	the quickest
wonderful	more wonderful	the most wonderful
amazing	more amazing	the most amazing
good	better	the best
bad	worse	the worst

2

2. the longest day
3. the hottest day
4. the cheapest model
5. the sweetest people
6. the nearest town
7. the most delicious lunch

3

Dear Ben and Jean,
  We're back from our trip to Britain now. It

most wonderful

was our ~~wonderfulest~~ trip ever, and Scotland was the ~~most~~ prettiest part of the trip. Thanks so much for all your help. We're so happy you came along when you did. The next time we

cheapest

take a vacation we won't rent the ~~most cheap~~ model, and we won't rent from that company

worst

again. It's the ~~worse~~ rental company we know of. No spare tire—how ridiculous! Actually,

most

it was the ˄ridiculous thing that happened on the trip.
  Thanks also for that wonderful lunch. It was

best

the ~~most good~~ meal we had on the whole trip. We hope to take you to a nice restaurant in Seattle sometime. Do you have any plans to come to this part of the world?
Best,
Amanda and Josh Wang

4

1. the newest
2. the most valuable
3. the biggest
4. the oldest
5. the most artistic
6. the most colorful

UNIT 30 Prepositions of Time: In, On, At

(pages 232–238)

Working Together
B.

The Big Rock Concert is on Wednesday, the 24th of May, at 7:30 P.M.

This Week's Basketball Game is on Monday, the 22nd of May, at 6:45 P.M.

The Drama Club's New Play is on Tuesday, the 23rd of May, at 8:00 P.M.

The Volleyball Club Party is on Sunday, the 21st of May, at 7:00 P.M.

1

on the 20th, at 2:30, on Sunday afternoon, on Saturday

2

2. in
3. at
4. at
5. at
6. in
7. at
8. on
9. in

3

1. **B.** Dinner is usually at 7:00 or 7:30.
2. **A.** What time do people start work in the morning?
   B. People usually start work at 8:00.
3. **A.** What do people do in the evenings?
   B. They often watch TV in the evenings.
4. **A.** What do people do on weekends?
   B. They often visit friends on weekends.

4

on

1. Daniela is leaving Seattle ~~in~~ Monday,

at

January 25, ~~on~~ 12:00 noon.

2. Her flight arrives in Chicago ~~in~~ *at* 6:00 ~~at~~ *in* the evening.

3. Her flight to London leaves at 7:30 ~~in the~~ *at* night.

4. Flight 774 arrives in London ~~in~~ *at* 11:30 ~~on~~ *in* the morning.

5. Her flight to Bucharest leaves ~~in~~ *at* 2:00 P.M. ~~in~~ *on* January 26.

6. It arrives in Bucharest at 6:05 ~~at~~ *in the* evening.

5 |

Day, month, and date Felix leaves Seattle	Time first flight leaves Seattle	Time second flight leaves Seattle	Day, month, and date Felix returns to Seattle
on Thursday, January 30th	at noon	at 6:30 in the evening	on Friday, February 7th

UNIT 31 The Future with *Be going to*: Statements
(pages 242–247)

1 |

1. Josh, do I need my heavy coat? *e*
2. Mom, what are we going to have for dinner? *f*
3. Dad, where's Mom going? *d*
4. Do you think Mark and Kathy are going to get married? *b*
5. What's going to happen next June? *c*
6. Does Jason have a serious girlfriend? *a*

a. Yes, he's going to see her tonight.
b. Probably. They're a great couple.
c. Judy's going to graduate.
d. To the store. We're out of milk.
e. Yes. It's going to snow.
f. We're going to have steak.

2 |

2. is going to be
3. is going to attend
4. is going to invite
5. is going to take
6. are going to videotape
7. are going to go
8. is going to win
9. is going to play

3 |

2. is going to finish
3. aren't going to win
4. are going to win
5. isn't going to lose
6. isn't going to win
7. is going to win
8. isn't going to finish

4 |

Dear Kathy,

I hope you're going *to* be in town Sunday evening. Josh and I are *going to* have a little party to watch the big game on TV. We are going *to* have pizza and dessert. We ~~be~~ *are* going to start the meal about 5:00. I think the game ~~are~~ *is* going to start at 6:00. Please come if you can. But can you let us know? We *are* going to be out of town until Tuesday. Call after that, OK?
        Amanda

5 |

1. F **2.** T **3.** F **4.** F **5.** T **6.** NI **7.** T **8.** T

UNIT 32 The Future with *Be going to*: Yes / No Questions
(pages 248–254)

1 |

g **2.** Are we going to (be) late?
a **3.** Is the soccer game going to (be) in the park?
f **4.** Do they (go) to the movies every week?
e **5.** Are they going to (win)?
c **6.** Is she going to (work) tomorrow?
d **7.** Are you going to (have) pizza?

2 |

2. had, 're having, Are . . . going to have, 're going to have
3. wear, wore, 're wearing, Are . . . going to wear
4. watched, are . . . watching, 'm going to watch
5. 's going to cook, 'm going to cook, cooked

3

A. 2. Is it going to mean a lot of work
   3. Are the children going to be OK
   4. Is Tim going to spend more time at home
B. 5. Is Jessica going to change
   6. Is Jessica going to work all the time
   7. Are we going to have time together
   8. Is Jessica going to earn more than I do

4

2. Hi, honey. I forgot my date book. ~~Is~~ *Are* Fred and Janet going to meet us at 8:00 or 8:30? Please call.

3. This message is for Jessica Olson. This is George Selig. Is the conference going ^*to* start on the 6th or the 7th?

4. Hi, Mom. I'm not going to be home until 9:00. Al and I ~~am~~ *are* going to study together.

5

1. No	**4.** No Information
2. No	**5.** No
3. Yes	**6.** Yes

8

Possible answers:

The man and woman in the car are going to play tennis. They are going to get a parking ticket.

The pickpocket is going to steal the woman's wallet.

The people are going to the movies.

The mother and child are going to see the cartoon.

UNIT 33 The Future with *Be going to: Wh-* Questions *(pages 255–260)*

1

1. Mom, (what time are we going to have dinner?) *d*
   a. Jeremy is, Dad.
   b. Yes, for about a month.
2. Are they ever going to get married? *c*
   c. Yes. <u>The wedding's going to be in June.</u>
3. (What are you going to do tonight,) Steve? *e*
   d. At six o'clock sharp.
   e. <u>I'm going to watch a video.</u>

4. (Why are you going to sell your car,) Judy? *f*
   f. It's always in the shop.
5. (Who's going to do the dishes tonight,) kids? *a*
6. Are you going to be away very long? *b*

2

2. Where is it going to be
3. Where are you going to go
4. How much is that going to cost
5. How long are you going to be
6. What places are you going to visit
7. Where are you going to live
8. Who's going to win

3

1. B: Jeremy ^*'s* going to do them, Mom. I did them last night.

2. A: Amanda, how many people ^*are* we ~~are~~ going to invite?
   B: I think about eight.

3. A: Where ~~Mark and Kathy are~~ *are Mark and Kathy* going to go on their honeymoon?
   B: They're going to go to India.

4. A: What time is ~~going to start the party~~ *the party going to start*?
   B: It's going to start at about 5:30.

5. A: How ~~the weather is~~ *is the weather* going to be on Saturday?
   B: The weatherman says ^*it* is going to be sunny and warm.

4

1. What are we going to eat?
2. Why are we going to have milk?
3. What time are we going to have dinner?
4. When is the game going to start?
5. Who's going to call the people?

Using the PowerPoint® presentations

The PowerPoint presentations are saved as .PPS files, which means that they open in Slide Show view and cannot be edited. The instructions in this section explain the basic steps of opening and using the PowerPoint presentations.

2.1. Start a Presentation

2.1.1. Windows

- Insert the PowerPoint® presentations CD-ROM into the CD-ROM drive. On most computers, a Contents page will open automatically.
- If the Contents page does not open automatically, open **My Computer**, double-click on the CD-ROM drive, and then double-click on the "**Start.html**" file.
- On the Contents page, click the link for "**PowerPoint presentations.**"
- Click the link for the presentation you wish to view.

2.1.2. Macintosh

- Insert the PowerPoint® presentations CD-ROM into the CD-ROM drive.
- Double-click on the CD-ROM drive icon, the symbol that looks like a CD.
- Double-click on the "**Start.html**" file.
- On the Contents page, click the link for "**PowerPoint presentations.**"
- Click the link for the presentation you wish to view.

2.2. Advance Through Slides

To advance from one slide to the next or from one animation to the next, click the left mouse button, the **Down Arrow** button (⬇) or the **Right Arrow** button (➡) on the keyboard.

2.3. Go Back Through Slides

To go back to previous slides, or to go back through the animations on a slide, click the **Up Arrow** button (⬆) or the **Left Arrow** button (⬅) on the keyboard.

2.4. Exit a Presentation

Press the "**Esc**" (escape) button on the keyboard.

Technical Support

For Technical Support, email
EPSupport@pearsoned.com

License Agreement

READ THIS LICENSE CAREFULLY BEFORE OPENING THIS PACKAGE. BY OPENING THIS PACKAGE, YOU ARE AGREEING TO THE TERMS AND CONDITIONS OF THIS LICENSE. IF YOU DO NOT AGREE, DO NOT OPEN THE PACKAGE. PROMPTLY RETURN THE UNOPENED PACKAGE AND ALL ACCOMPANYING ITEMS TO THE PLACE YOU OBTAINED THEM. *THESE TERMS APPLY TO ALL LICENSED SOFTWARE ON THE DISK EXCEPT THAT THE TERMS FOR USE OF ANY SHAREWARE OR FREEWARE ON THE DISKETTES ARE AS SET FORTH IN THE ELECTRONIC LICENSE LOCATED ON THE DISK:*

1. **GRANT OF LICENSE and OWNERSHIP:** The enclosed data disk ("Software") is licensed, not sold, to you by Pearson Education, Inc. Publishing as Pearson Longman ("We" or the "Company") for academic purposes and in consideration of your purchase or adoption of the accompanying Company textbooks and/or other materials, and your agreement to these terms. This license allows instructors teaching the course using the Company textbook that accompanies this Software (the "Focus on Grammar") to use, and display the data on a single computer (i.e., with a single CPU) at a single location for academic use only, so long as you comply with the terms of this Agreement.

   We reserve any rights not granted to you. You own only the disk(s) but we and our licensors own the Software itself.

2. **RESTRICTIONS ON USE AND TRANSFER:** You may not transfer, distribute or make available the Software or the Documentation, except to instructors and students in your school in connection with the Course. You may not reverse engineer, disassemble, decompile, modify, adapt, translate or create derivative works based on the Software or the Documentation. You may be held legally responsible for any copying or copyright infringement that is caused by your failure to abide by the terms of these restrictions.

3. **TERMINATION:** This license is effective until terminated. This license will terminate automatically without notice from the Company if you fail to comply with any provisions or limitations of this license. Upon termination, you shall destroy the Documentation and all copies of the Software. All provisions of this Agreement as to limitation and disclaimer of warranties, limitation of liability, remedies or damages, and our ownership rights shall survive termination.

4. **DISCLAIMER OF WARRANTY: THE COMPANY AND ITS LICENSORS MAKE NO WARRANTIES ABOUT THE SOFTWARE, WHICH IS PROVIDED "AS-IS." IF THE DISK IS DEFECTIVE IN MATERIALS OR WORKMANSHIP, YOUR ONLY REMEDY IS TO RETURN IT TO THE COMPANY WITHIN 30 DAYS FOR REPLACEMENT UNLESS THE COMPANY DETERMINES IN GOOD FAITH THAT THE DISK HAS BEEN MISUSED OR IMPROPERLY INSTALLED, REPAIRED, ALTERED OR DAMAGED. THE COMPANY DISCLAIMS ALL WARRANTIES, EXPRESS OR IMPLIED, INCLUDING WITHOUT LIMITATION, THE IMPLIED WARRANTIES OF MERCHANTABILITY AND FITNESS FOR A PARTICULAR PURPOSE. THE COMPANY DOES NOT WARRANT, GUARANTEE OR MAKE ANY REPRESENTATION REGARDING THE ACCURACY, RELIABILITY, CURRENTNESS, USE, OR RESULTS OF USE, OF THE SOFTWARE.**

5. **LIMITATION OF REMEDIES AND DAMAGES: IN NO EVENT, SHALL THE COMPANY OR ITS EMPLOYEES, AGENTS, LICENSORS OR CONTRACTORS BE LIABLE FOR ANY INCIDENTAL, INDIRECT, SPECIAL OR CONSEQUENTIAL DAMAGES ARISING OUT OF OR IN CONNECTION WITH THIS LICENSE OR THE SOFTWARE, INCLUDING, WITHOUT LIMITATION, LOSS OF USE, LOSS OF DATA, LOSS OF INCOME OR PROFIT, OR OTHER LOSSES SUSTAINED AS A RESULT OF INJURY TO ANY PERSON, OR LOSS OF OR DAMAGE TO PROPERTY, OR CLAIMS OF THIRD PARTIES, EVEN IF THE COMPANY OR AN AUTHORIZED REPRESENTATIVE OF THE COMPANY HAS BEEN ADVISED OF THE POSSIBILITY OF SUCH DAMAGES.** SOME JURISDICTIONS DO NOT ALLOW THE LIMITATION OF DAMAGES IN CERTAIN CIRCUMSTANCES, SO THE ABOVE LIMITATIONS MAY NOT ALWAYS APPLY.

6. **GENERAL:** THIS AGREEMENT SHALL BE CONSTRUED IN ACCORDANCE WITH THE LAWS OF THE UNITED STATES OF AMERICA AND THE STATE OF NEW YORK, APPLICABLE TO CONTRACTS MADE IN NEW YORK, EXCLUDING THE STATE'S LAWS AND POLICIES ON CONFLICTS OF LAW, AND SHALL BENEFIT THE COMPANY, ITS AFFILIATES AND ASSIGNEES. This Agreement is the complete and exclusive statement of the agreement between you and the Company and supersedes all proposals, prior agreements, oral or written, and any other communications between you and the Company or any of its representatives relating to the subject matter. If you are a U.S. Government user, this Software is licensed with "restricted rights" as set forth in subparagraphs (a)-(d) of the Commercial Computer-Restricted Rights clause at FAR 52.227-19 or in subparagraphs (c)(1)(ii) of the Rights in Technical Data and Computer Software clause at DFARS 252.227-7013, and similar clauses, as applicable.

Notes